PHYSICAL EDUCATION FOR BLIND CHILDREN

Ғʀᴏɴᴛɪsᴘɪᴇᴄᴇ

Guide wires for blind runners. TOP: Massachusetts; MIDDLE: California;
BOTTOM: Pennsylvania.

PHYSICAL EDUCATION FOR BLIND CHILDREN

By

CHARLES E. BUELL, Ed.D.

Athletic Director
California School for the Blind
Berkeley, California

With Forewords by

Genevie Dexter

California State Department of Education
Sacramento, California

and

James R. Bancroft

Berkeley, California

CHARLES C THOMAS • PUBLISHER
Springfield • Illinois • U.S.A.

Published and Distributed Throughout the World by
CHARLES C THOMAS • PUBLISHER
BANNERSTONE HOUSE
301-327 East Lawrence Avenue, Springfield, Illinois, U.S.A.
NATCHEZ PLANTATION HOUSE
735 North Atlantic Boulevard, Fort Lauderdale, Florida, U.S.A.

*With THOMAS BOOKS careful attention is given to all details of
manufacturing and design. It is the Publisher's desire to present books
that are satisfactory as to their physical qualities and artistic possibilities
and appropriate for their particular use. THOMAS BOOKS will be true
to those laws of quality that assure a good name and good will.*

To visually handicapped children whom
I have been able to inspire to improve themselves

FOREWORD

From a Physical Educator—

OPPORTUNITIES FOR VISUALLY handicapped boys and girls to be so educated that they may make their full contribution as citizens in the United States have increased many fold within the last two decades. Development of skills which will make possible co-ordinated movement in locomotion, physical fitness and success in physical activity and recreation is a vital ingredient of this education.

Leadership and source material for teaching physical education suitable for the visually handicapped at each age grouping have been needed. Charles E. Buell has stressed continuously the necessity for appropriate physical education programs for visually handicapped boys and girls in both residential and public schools. From his experience and education the author has compiled material which provides the concepts and teaching suggestions necessary for professional men and women to teach with empathy physical education to partially seeing and sightless pupils.

Parents, teachers and school administrators will find the principles described in *Physical Education for Blind Children* easy to apply. In applying these principles, parents, teachers and school administrators will assist visually handicapped boys and girls to advance toward full contribution and an abundant life.

Sacramento, California　　　GENEVIE DEXTER

Consultant in Physical Education
California State Department
of Education

From a Parent—

WE BELIEVE that a blind child needs, even more than a child with vision, a balanced, imaginative and active physical education and recreation program. This conclusion is based on experience with our blind son (now age fourteen) and his friends, some blind and some not.

Active physical sports should begin before age one and continue for life. From the first gentle balancing act with a baby, each new game or sport builds upon the old. Sometimes skills develop slowly, but each success adds confidence. Some blind children seem to be born athletes, some quite the opposite, and, of course, most are in between. All have one problem in common—they cannot learn merely by watching others. An effective physical education program will offer everyone the stimulus and opportunity to develop to capacity and have fun along the way.

Human beings seem to need to prove to themselves that they can get along in the world. Blindness can become a refuge in which to hide or a challenge to meet and to surmount by the standards of a seeing world. A young blind adult has already gone far toward either joining or withdrawing from the world. A sound physical education program will spur both the choice and the ability to participate. Over a period of years he learns to try, to win, to lose, to plunge into a team effort, to face unknowns, to control himself physically and mentally and to enjoy an easy comradeship with others.

Now let's look at the reactions of a sighted world. If the blind child is always on the sidelines, his seeing peers can easily conclude that blind people are by definition helpless and disqualified from having fun. If he is a frequent and active participant, he has a chance to earn acceptance on his merits as a human being. There will always be games in which he cannot effectively compete, but the alternative should be another activity and not the sidelines. Active integration of blind children into physical education programs is therefore an important early step toward ultimate social and economic integration of blind adults.

Dr. Buell's book, like his previous writings, distills facts and viewpoints from his years of work with a great many blind children. He is a serious scholar, a concise writer and a tireless teacher. The resulting book is thorough, authoritative, interesting and, best of all, encouraging.

Berkeley, California　　　　　　　　　JAMES R. BANCROFT

PREFACE

T HIS textbook has been written especially for teachers and administrators in the public schools and also the residential schools for the blind, for parents of visually handicapped children, for students planning to teach physical education, for hospitals with rehabilitation departments and for blind boys and girls in high school and college. A well-rounded program of vigorous physical education for blind children is described in detail. Many activities are not modified, but, of course, others must be modified somewhat to be of most value to sightless pupils.

The author vigorously opposes the policy followed by some public schools which results in excusing many thousands of blind chlidren from physical education. Perhaps such a policy is due to the mistaken notion that these pupils need more protection than the rest of the student body. In reality, those who are not permitted to leave the sidelines are being denied the right to achieve the fullest possible development of which they are capable. Schools should strive to offer handicapped children programs which will emphasize their abilities instead of their disabilities. Such programs will bring blind boys and girls closer to their seeing peers instead of widening the gap.

The approach of the author is a practical one, based upon his twenty-five years of experience as a teacher of blind children. In this book, therefore, practice receives more attention than theory. Some problems are present in such an approach. First, information on blind boys and girls is very difficult to collect because they are so widely separated. Although much effort was expanded in gathering as many facts as possible, it is likely that some valuable information has not come to the attention of the author. Second, most of the experience in teaching physical education to blind children has been gained in residential schools. This will explain why somewhat more space is devoted to physical education in residential schools than in public schools. Third, many residential schools offer much more physical education to blind boys than girls. Because of this, somewhat more attention is given to activities for boys. The author hastens to point out that these are practical matters and have nothing to do with theory. Actually, physical education is of equal importance to girls and boys and to blind pupils, regardless of whether they attend public schools or residential schools.

It is possible the reader will use this book as a reference and not concern himself with every chapter. With this in mind, and due to the fact that activities have been approached from different points of view, there is a bit of repetition. In this way the reader will probably not miss the concepts considered to be of utmost importance.

ACKNOWLEDGMENTS

ACKNOWLEDGMENT IS MADE and appreciation expressed for the help received from others in the preparation of this book. Special acknowledgment is made to Genevie Dexter, Consultant in Physical Education for the State of California, for reading the manuscript and making many valuable criticisms. For information furnished, the author is indebted to Robert Allman, a blind Philadelphia attorney; Leroy Price, Secretary of the American Blind Bowling Association; Dr. George Anderson, Associate Executive Secretary of the American Association of Health, Physical Education and Recreation; Dr. Anna Espenschade, Head of the Department of Physical Education for Women at the University of California at Berkeley; James Burton of the American Printing House for the Blind; Mr. Arthur Keller, Manager, Sales Division, American Foundation for the Blind; John Stewart, Product Manager, Voit Rubber Corporation; Maurice Olsen, formerly Secretary of the American Association of Instructors of the Blind; Claude Ellis, Assistant Principal, Perkins School for the Blind; Dr. Robert Thompson, Superintendent of the Michigan School for the Blind; Dr. D. W. Overbeay, Superintendent, Ohio School for the Blind; Dr. Berthold Lowenfeld, formerly Superintendent of the California School for the Blind; V. R. Carter, Superintendent, Oklahoma School for the Blind; Jerry Regler, Superintendent, Nebraska School for the Visually Handicapped; B. Q. Scruggs, Principal, Alabama School for the Blind; William English, Principal, Virginia School for the Blind; Joseph Kerr, Principal, Overbrook School for the Blind; Ernest Parmer, Principal, Kansas School for the Blind; W. C. Gill, Superintendent of the Louisiana School for the Blind; and J. M. Woolly, Superintendent of the Arkansas School for the Blind. Physical educators of the blind to whom the author is particularly grateful are Roy Brothers, Ron Teubner, Charles Young, Sy Haliczer, Carol Wadell, Paul Tapia,

Roger Davis, Al Eberhardt, William Evans, Francis Hetherington and Robert Roy.

Others to whom the author is indebted are Joe Reynolds and Charles Weir of the Michigan School for the Blind and Bob McQuie of the Missouri School for the Blind. A particular thanks is due to James Bancroft for his parent's viewpoint. The writer wishes to thank his wife, Mrs. Josephine L. Buell, for her untiring assistance and many helpful literary criticisms.

Schools which have made photographs and school papers available to the author are thanked for their courteous and generous service.

C.E.B.

CONTENTS

PHYSICAL EDUCATION
FOR BLIND CHILDREN

Chapter 1

THE BLIND CHILD
AND PHYSICAL EDUCATION

STUDENTS WITH VERY MARKED deviations in vision form a very small percentage of the total school population. However, in numbers this group is large enough to be of real concern. Today in the United States there are over 18,000 children who are so visually handicapped that they read either Braille or large type books to gain their education. About 60 per cent of them are attending public schools, while the rest attend residential schools for the blind. A child should attend the type of school which can best meet his needs, be it public or residential. Some youngsters develop best by being in both environments at different periods of their childhood.

Although much progress has been made in the education of visually handicapped children, improvements in some areas have not kept pace. For example, many blind boys and girls have been denied the opportunity to fully develop their physical capabilities. Loss of sight may tend to curtail physical activities in some ways, but the chief difficulty is the attitude of the public toward blindness. This attitude usually emphasizes overprotection rather than the development of physical and mental potentials. The distribution of accurate information on a subject results in the development of desirable attitudes. It is hoped this book will assist in developing a better understanding of the physical abilities of blind children.

Another hindrance to progress has been the false assumption that individuals with visual impairments are prone to more accidents and injuries than are others. Actually accidents and injuries are not any more common among blind children than elsewhere, nor should they be of any more concern. Over 130 years ago, Dr. Samuel Gridley Howe said: "Do not too much re-

3

gard bumps upon the forehead, rough scratches or bloody noses, even these may have their good influences. At the worst, they affect only the bark, and do not injure the system like the rust of inaction." Dr. Howe was a pioneer in the education of blind children.

Most physical education of visually handicapped children has been carried on in residential schools for the blind. This is to be expected, because it has been only within the last twenty years that more than 10 per cent of visually handicapped boys and girls have attended public schools. For this reason, most writings on the subject, including this book, tend to emphasize what has been successfully practiced. It should not be implied that vigorous physical education cannot be carried on for blind children in the public schools. In Chapter 4 will be found one of the first and most detailed discussions to appear on such a program—a program which should include pupils with little or no vision, as well as those who are sight-saving cases.

Today, blind children, guided by understanding parents, teachers and recreation leaders, are participating more in physical activities available in the school and community. Some of these activities are swimming, rowing, bowling, camping, hiking, tandem cycling, water cycling, water skiing, roller skating, ice skating, dancing, riding horses and winter sports.

HOW MUCH DO BLIND CHILDREN NEED PHYSICAL EDUCATION?

The future belongs to the physically fit, whether it be in factory work, salesmanship or in professional work. The future belongs to those vigorous enough to live it. Medical authorities put it this way: "It is a tragic waste to highly educate the minds of our children and neglect the physical conditioning that can help them participate in the future to the full extent of their abilities."

Physical fitness is important for all of us, but particularly for blind individuals. Superior stamina is required by visually handicapped persons in carrying on day-to-day activities and functioning in social situations, where they are usually under abnormal pressure. A blind person must expend much more energy to reach the same rung of success as an individual who has normal vision. This belief has been expressed by many outstanding educators of blind children. Dr. Edward Waterhouse, Director of Perkins School for the Blind, has written: "Adult life makes greater physical demands on the blind than it does on the seeing." Therefore, physical education is even more important for blind individuals than it is for others. This must be kept in mind if children are to develop into happy and useful citizens. Today, the expectation is that most blind children will become successfully employed as adults and become assets to their communities.

Regardless of limitations in budget, facilities or physical handicap, we must provide our children, including those who are blind, the daily minimum of vigorous exercise they need for adequate physical development.

AIDS TO TEACHERS

When the American Association of Instructors of the Blind introduced workshop sessions in the convention program in 1952, many areas of education of blind children were stimulated. Certainly the teachers who have attended the physical education workshops held biennially have received much of value from them. By reading the summaries of these workshops, other physical educators have gained practical knowledge. The *Bulletin for Physical Educators of the Blind*[1] was discussed at the first workshop and has been published three times a year since that time.

In the summer of 1964 the first extended workshop for physical educators of the blind was sponsored by the American Association of Instructors of the Blind and by Michigan State University. It was held in the large new physical education plant of the Michigan School for the Blind. In addition to papers and discussions by leaders in the field, blind children participated in a wide variety of physical education activities on a laboratory basis. The emphasis during the two-week workshop was placed upon practical application of subject matter. It is likely this stimulating development will lead to more summer workshops for physical educators of blind children. It is hoped federal funds will become available for use in such institutes.

---

1. For information write to the American Association of Instructors of the Blind, 2363 South Spring Avenue, St. Louis 10, Missouri.

In recent years a number of universities and colleges have added a course on adapted physical education to the training of prospective physical educators. These courses usually include some discussion of physical education for blind children.

A silent film on physical education of blind children has been available for twelve years. During 1964 a sound film on the same subject was released.[2] Motion pictures have contributed much to education.

Recently a bibliography on physical education for blind children was prepared by a committee of physical educators of the blind. It is available from the American Association of Instructors of the Blind. A pamphlet entitled *A Swimming Program for Blind Children*[3] by Belenky, offers many helpful suggestions for teaching swimming.

Two of Buell's pamphlets, *Recreation for the Blind*[4] and *Motor Performance of Visually Handicapped Children*,[5] are valuable teaching aids.

Teachers who wish more information on physical education tests for blind boys than is contained in Chapters 11 and 12 will find an article by Haliczer[6] valuable.

For instructors interested in teaching dancing, two articles which appeared in the *International Journal for the Education of the Blind* are worth mentioning: (a) MORGAN, MYRA, Square dancing in a school for the blind, Vol. VI: No. 2, December, 1956; and (b) A program of dance for visually handicapped young people. A symposium. Vol VII: No. 3, March, 1958.

Physical educators are likely to be involved in camping programs of the school, and other teachers should be familiar with the activities and their goals. A monograph by Frampton and

2. Charles Buell, California School for the Blind, 3001 Derby Street, Berkeley, California.

3. BELENKY, ROBERT: *A Swimming Program For Blind Children.* New York, American Foundation for the Blind, 1955, 44 pp.

4. BUELL, CHARLES:*Recreation for the Blind.* New York, American Foundation for the Blind, 1951, 40 pp.

5. BUELL, CHARLES: *Motor Performance of Visually Handicapped Children.* Ann Arbor, Michigan, Edwards Brothers, 1950, 125 pp.

6. HALICZER, S. L.: Physical education tests for boys. *International Journal for Education of the Blind,* May, 1959, pp. 129-133.

Mitchell[7] gives a detailed description of Camp Wapanacki, one of the well-known camps for blind children.

From time to time, books on sports and physical education for the handicapped have appeared. One of the more recent books in this field is Fait's *Adapted Physical Education*,[8] which includes a discussion on blindness.

The teaching aids mentioned above are helpful. It is obvious that many more will be needed before the program of physical education for blind children becomes adequate.

Physical education for visually handicapped youngsters is a very specialized field, requiring much knowledge and understanding. For this reason, an advisory or consultant service could fill a very definite need, particularly in public schools. Consultants in physical education of the blind should be employed by the United States Office of Education, the Departments of Education of all larger states and some of the most populous cities. These consultants would be available to discuss the problems involved and answer questions. They would visit schools and could put on demonstrations if asked to do so. Such a service would encourage many schools to start a physical education program for their students with impaired vision, and it would stimulate the improvement of existing programs.

AIDS TO BLIND CHILDREN

There has been very little information on physical education available to Braille readers. Recently, some attempts have been made to overcome this shortage. At the request of the American Association of Instructors of the Blind, the book *Physical Education for High School Students* was put into Braille by the American Printing House for the Blind in 1958. The book lists the rules and describes the strategy of a wide variety of games and sports. Two more useful books have recently become available in Braille and large type[9]—*The Boys' Book of Physical Fitness and The Girls'*

7. FRAMPTON, M. E., and MITCHELL, PAUL C.: *Camping for Blind Youth.* New York, New York Institute for the Blind, 1949, 139 pp.

8. FAIT, HOLLIS: *Adapted Physical Education.* Philadelphia, W. B. Saunders, 1960, pp. 133-151.

9. The American Printing House for the Blind, 1839 Frankfort Avenue, Louisville 6, Kentucky.

Book of Physical Fitness, written by Hal and Jean Vermes. A sports column in *Teen-time,*[10] a magazine available in Braille and large type,[9] emphasizes activities of blind athletes. The column has brought inspiration to visually handicapped boys and girls in all parts of the United States.

In 1956 three blind students were awarded scholarships for proficiency in wrestling and academic achievement by Auburn University, Maryland University and New Mexico University, and since that time other athletic scholarships have been granted to blind wrestlers. Two of the recipients of these scholarships are now highly respected physical educators of blind children.

AIMS AND OBJECTIVES

The aims and objectives of a physical education program for blind children should be those of the public schools of the state. In some cases, more emphasis will be placed upon certain objectives and less on others. There are a few aims of the program that result from blindness itself.

As already mentioned, additional emphasis should be placed upon the development of physical fitness, so that a blind individual can better meet the unusual demands of daily living made upon him.

More than usual emphasis should be placed upon activities which will enable blind children to participate in family and community recreation and exercise. It is important that a visually handicapped pupil expand his opportunities to participate with and gain recognition from sighted peers in play situations.

Even more emphasis than usual will encourage the development of sport skills for more worthy use of leisure time. Two reasons why this is important are: (a) more blind people have more leisure time than do those who have normal vision; (b) most visually handicapped people tend to be sedentary.

Another aim is to equip the student with a knowledge of his disability and the extent to which it limits his activities. Blindness results in a need for orientation and mobility. The physical education class is one place where much valuable training can be

---

10. Free subscriptions available from Concordia Publishing House, 3558 South Jefferson Avenue, St. Louis, Missouri.

given. This includes learning to use clues of sound, odor, direction of wind or sun, terrain under foot, etc. Much emphasis should be placed upon rapid movement using available clues.

Since fear is found oftener in blind children, much stress should be placed upon overcoming this frame of mind, especially in the primary and elementary grades. Children should be encouraged to run rapidly and to enter water of a depth comparable to their swimming abilities. Activities should be stressed that will assist the visually handicapped child to overcome fear.

Activities must be selected that will not neglect the blind in favor of the partially seeing or sighted children. If sightless boys and girls are to take an active part in a program which includes children with some or all their vision, careful planning is absolutely necessary.

An aim that should not be overlooked is that of imparting knowledge of various sports, some of which may not be practical for sightless players. It is important that visually handicapped children be able to use this information as a basis for conversation with their peers, even though they may not participate. This will improve the interest and understanding of sports telecasts and radio broadcasts and also stimulate attendance at sporting events. A national football prediction contest has been conducted for 500 blind students annually for many years in order to increase their interest in the sport.

SPECIAL METHODS

First, a teacher must be really interested in his task, because adequately instructing blind boys and girls requires unusually hard work and extra patience. When teaching new stunts or exercises, it is often necessary for the leader to perform the exercise, while the hands of the sightless examine the parts of the body involved. Sometimes the feet and arms of a blind child should be moved by the teacher to show correct form. When one student is receiving individual attention, the others should have something definite to do.

During the progress of a game, an instructor should verbally describe the essentials. All children should be kept posted on the game situations. If you were sightless, what would you want to know? This can be the teacher's guide. However, this must be done in an intelligent manner. A sympathetic or condescending attitude is very undesirable and harmful.

When conducting races across a field, a whistle should be blown in front of the contestants to give them direction. For boys, in some contact games, one team should remove shirts, so that identification will be made easier for sightless players.

Outdoor relays are best set up with a turning point at the edge of a surface. For example, the edge of grass along a running track or sidewalk serves as a good turning point. Indoor relays are best run on oblong mats, one mat provided for each team. Mats enable players to keep their direction and make quick turns at the right time.

Teaching the correct rhythm for jumping rope is often difficult. One practical method is to have the pupil stand behind the teacher and place his hands on the hips or shoulders of the instructor. After they have practiced jumping together, a rope can be introduced, first by the instructor making the rope movements and then by the child.

Lines on playing fields should be clearly marked in bright colors. Even children with little more than light perception can follow white lines on green grass.

Of course, charts, team lists, schedules, bowling averages, rules, etc. should be written in Braille or large type. These can be distributed or posted on the bulletin board.

Physical education classes for the visually handicapped should not exceed fifteen children. If much individual work is to be done, the class size should be reduced, or a second adult should be present to assist. This is particularly necessary in swimming classes where beginners are being given instruction.

SPECIAL EQUIPMENT

The number of items which have been specially developed for use in classes for physical education of blind children is quite limited. With the technical knowledge available to develop spacecraft, computers, etc., it seems that more such equipment should have been built to aid sightless youngsters in their play.

One device which has been available for a long time is the

guide wire. Guide wires enable blind boys and girls to run at top speed without fear. One can also run back and forth to build up his endurance. A student grasps a short rope which is tied to a metal ring that slides along a wire stretched 100 yds. without intervening supports.

There are some recordings available which can assist blind children in their home exercise programs. The records, *Physical Fitness and You,* by Bonnie Prudden, a well-known exercise consultant, may be borrowed from the Regional Libraries for the Blind or purchased from the American Foundation for the Blind, 15 West 16th Street, New York 11, New York.

A visually handicapped boy or girl scout or a leader may obtain, without charge, a Braille First Aid Manual from the Christian Executive Braille Foundation, 4444 South 52nd Street, Lincoln, Nebraska 68516.

A valuable device was made available in 1965 by the American Printing House for the Blind in Louisville. It is an audible goal-locator which can be used to advantage in basketball goal shooting. The locator can also be used to assist in the location of bases or goals in other games. In addition, it can provide orientation in an indoor swimming pool or in other places.

The audible goal-locator is housed in a plywood box. The device can be used outdoors, but should be taken in when not in use. The locator is a motor-driven noisemaker which emits clicking sounds at about 150 pulses per minute. The cord should be plugged into a 116-volt, 60-cycle current. A similar device has been used at Perkins for many years and has proved very practical. Little maintenance is required. The price of the audible goal-locator is $18.50, plus express on 11 lbs from Louisville to destination.

One of the greatest needs in physical education of blind children is a practical audible ball. Efforts are being made to design such a ball, but so far those that have been developed have disadvantages—some of them rather serious. After much experimentation, the Royal National Institute for the Blind[11] in England placed an audible ball on the market five years ago, and it was tried in

---

11. Royal National Institute for the Blind, 224 Great Portland Street, London, W. 1., England. The price of the ball is $17.30.

a number of schools in the United States but found to have limited value. It has an audible "beeper" made possible by a rechargeable dry cell. The sound has a frequency of 3,000 cycles per second, which is difficult to hear under play conditions. An oscillator with 2,000 cycles per second has been found by the American Printing House for the Blind to be much more practical. The English ball will not withstand kicking or batting, and does not have a true bounce. At the present time the APH is experimenting with the possibility of placing a 4-oz oscillator in the center of a basketball or soccer ball. Different types of webbing to suspend the oscillator have been tried without success. It is uncertain when or if this difficult problem can be solved at a reasonable cost. In the meantime, the English ball is being successfully used for such games as snatch the bacon, spud, call ball, circle numbers and for orientation activities.

At the International Conference on the Education of Blind Youth, American educators became aware of the fact that bell balls were being manufactured in Germany,[12] and a number of schools and classes for the blind in the United States have purchased them. They are rather heavy and do not bounce very high or for long, but they withstand kicking and batting. The German ball has been successfully used for baseball, kick baseball and various forms of kickball games. It has the advantage of being economical. When a bell ball is bouncing or rolling, it can be caught by totally blind fielders, and this factor has made their part in some games much more active. However, the bells are useless when the ball comes to rest.

During 1964, the Voit Rubber Corporation of Santa Ana, California, following the writer's suggestions, manufactured a durable yellow soccer ball with a bell inside, similar to the German ball. It withstands kicking, and when the batter places one knee on the ground, endures batting. Since the Voit Corporation did not wish to handle retail sales of the ball, the writer sought another distributor. The American Printing House for the Blind was very much interested in the project, but a clause in its charter requires that all items sold by them must be manufactured in its own

---

12. Vereln zur Forderung der Blindenbildung, 3 Hannover-Kerchrode, Bleekstrasse 26, Germany. Soccer ball about $3.50; smaller ball, $2.50.

plant. However, the American Foundation for the Blind, 15 West 16th Street, New York, New York, agreed to offer the bell ball for sale at a price of $5.90, including postage. The ball is being manufactured and distributed at cost, so that blind children will be able to play many games better. Even without a bell, a ball of this durability cannot be purchased at this price.

A new type of bicycle for blind persons, which might be called a "bicycle merry-go-round," was introduced seven years ago.[13] A bicycle is attached to each end of the bars, making it possible for blind persons to ride alone without danger of collision. At

FIGURE 1. A blind bowler at the Ohio State School for the blind.

---

13. Dr. Frank Dudley, President, Franklin Manufacturing Company, 12 Center Street, Westmont 7, New Jersey.

present, the cost of this device is rather high, but it has been made available to some blind children, mostly in schools and camps.

During the past ten years, gym scooters[14] have been in use by a number of children with impaired vision. They are made of 2 in. x 12 in. x 14 in. boards with four casters for rollers. These scooters will travel in any direction, and they provide much enjoyment, as well as good exercise.

At least two schools, Perkins and Overbrook, have automatic pinsetters for bowling. Under these conditions, an electric device can be installed which, by touch, indicates the pins standing.

A portable aluminum bowling rail, nine feet long and three feet high, is available from the American Foundation for the Blind in New York at a cost of $16.30. The parts slide together quickly, and there are no attachments to the lane or return racks. Bowling balls are placed on the metal base for ballast. A carrying bag is provided with the rail, which can be used on any lane.

PHYSICAL EDUCATION MEANS SYSTEMATIC INSTRUCTION

The objectives of physical education may be grouped under the heading of physical fitness, skills, attitudes and knowledge. To obtain proper physical fitness, guidance is essential. Basic skills will develop correctly only if instruction is offered. A child must be helped to develop desirable knowledge of and attitudes toward himself and others. The development of these important qualities should not be left to chance. This is why free play cannot act as a substitute for physical education.

THE CHALLENGE

The general public takes the attitude that the visually handicapped should be shielded in every way, while in reality they crave to be useful, active citizens. The values to be obtained from a good program of physical education are worth a few bumps and bruises. Physical education can do much to aid the blind and partially seeing individual to adjust to society. Since there is a wide variety of suitable activities available for use by children who have visual impairments, it is only a question of using them. There are no problems in the physical education of blind young-

---

14. Titus Gym Scooter Co., Winfield, Kansas, 67156.

sters that cannot be solved by energetic and intelligent leadership. It is the duty of teachers and administrators to provide a program of education, mental and physical, that will round out a fuller life and bring more health, success and happiness to the visually handicapped in adulthood. The community has an obligation to provide an adequate education for all of its children, and this includes those who are blind.

Chapter 2

HISTORICAL DEVELOPMENT OF PHYSICAL EDUCATION FOR THE BLIND

A weak body weakens the soul—if you would develop the understanding of your pupil, develop the powers which his understanding is to govern; incessantly train his body. Make him strong and healthy, that you may make him wise and intelligent; make him work, run, cry out, always busied about something; let him be a man in strength, and then he will be one in reason.

ROUSSEAU

THE EIGHTEENTH CENTURY was a period of transition to modern social, political and educational ideals. Rousseau's *Emile* has had tremendous influence on educational thought. Rousseau was aware of the earlier writings of Locke on the importance of a sound mind in a sound body. The French educational theorist stressed the value of sports, while Locke had concerned himself primarily with hygiene. Putting many of these ideas into practice, Basedow opened a naturalistic school at Dessau in 1774. Basedow believed that normal physical growth is extremely important and that there are intellectual and moral values to be gained from playing games. He was a pioneer in physical education for the common school.

A publication of another eighteenth century philosopher, namely Diderot, probably led Valentin Haüy to establish the first class for blind students at Paris in 1784.[1] Vocational education was stressed. Besides being valuable for the future, it increased the activity of blind individuals and tended to decrease general lassitude.[2] The schools for the blind that were soon established in the British Isles also emphasized industrial training. Manual labor took the place of physical education in most schools for the blind until 1850.

The value of physical education was recognized in Germany

---

1. SIZERANNE, M.: *The Blind as Seen Through Blind Eyes.* P. 62.
2. FRENCH, R. S.: *From Homer to Helen Keller.* P. 96.

16

and Austria. A system of gymnastics was prepared especially for the blind, and nature excursions were an important part of the program.[3] This program did not influence education in American schools for the blind.

THE LEADERSHIP OF SAMUEL GRIDLEY HOWE

In the United States three schools for the blind were founded between 1830 and 1833 at Boston, New York and Philadelphia. In the early American schools stress was placed on religion and manual training. Only one school, Perkins Institution in Boston, made special provision for physical activity. Perkins was the leader in physical education for the blind for at least eighty years. This was due to its outstanding director, Dr. Samuel Gridley Howe. Howe was a physician and a champion of health. For the first eight years this physical education consisted of compulsory recreation in the open air. In one of the school's first reports Howe wrote: "Strict attention is paid to the health of the pupils and although the time during which they are occupied may seem long, it is so varied by music and by work, that it has no injurious effect. Every fair day the house and school room is closed upon the male pupils, once at least, and sometimes oftener; so that they are obliged to resort to exercise in the open air. Once a week every pupil has the opportunity of having a warm bath; and on all occasions they are required to keep clean."[4]

Three years later, Howe wrote:

"The blind are more liable to disease and early death than seeing pupils; partly because there are many cases where blindness is the partial effect of some general cause, which occasions constitutional infirmity; partly because in early life they do not take exercise enough to develop the force of the system; and partly, from habits and indolence, physical and mental, acquired in later life. Now the majority of our pupils were past the age of adolescence when they entered; and are, therefore, still liable to the effect of unfavorable causes put into operation before."

Great attention, however, is now paid to their physical health, and there is no doubt that where this attention can be given from

3. *Ibid.*, p. 179.
4. *Perkins Report*, 1834. P. 10

early life, the mortality of the blind will not differ much from that of seeing pupils. The pupils are required to be perfectly clean; the sleeping rooms and the school rooms are very well ventilated; their diet is simple, but healthy and ample; their hours of eating, study, exercise and sleeping are regular; in short, everything is done to promote health, though we still have to contend with almost insurmountable repugnance in the older ones, to taking sufficient exercise.[5]

Howe was the first American to point out that it is the duty of educators to see that blind children exercise all the muscles of their body. "It is, however, a duty that is seldom fully discharged, because it is one in which the efforts of the instructor are rarely seconded by the inclination of the pupil."[6]

Very early Howe recognized the cause and treatment of certain physical manifestations of nervousness which have become known as "blindisms" because there are always some cases in every school for the blind. "It is true, that during the period of childhood and early youth, nature furnishes such a stock of animal spirits as urges even the blind boy to physical action; but his desire for movement and exercise is more generally repressed than encouraged by those who have the charge of him; and as he cannot run freely about, he seeks to work off the stimulus by motion of his body and limbs without changing his place. Hence it is so common to see blind persons who have contracted habits of reeling backward and forward, or from side to side, twitching the head, or jerking some part of the body, habits which sometimes become inveterate, and which make the subject of them appear very awkward and uncouth to seeing persons."[7]

The social results of blindness are not so much an outgrowth of the condition itself as of the attitude of other persons in the environment. Through the years school authorities have issued lengthy instructions on how to care for the blind. In one hundred years there has been little improvement on the original work of Dr. Howe, who wrote: "Never check the motions of the child; follow him, and watch him to prevent any serious accidents, but

---

5. *Perkins Report,* 1837. **P.** 3.
6. *Perkins Report,* 1847. **P.** 6.
7. *Ibid.,* p. 5.

do not interfere unnecessarily; do not even remove obstacles which he would learn to avoid by tumbling over them a few times.

Teach him to jump rope, to swing weights, to raise his body by his arms, and to mingle, as far as possible in the rough sports of the older boys, and do not be apprehensive of his safety, and if you should see him clambering in the branches of a tree, be sure he is less likely to fall than if he had eyes.[8]

"Let a boy saw wood, take care of cattle, do jobs about the house, and if you can afford it, let him have a leader for long excursions, let him learn to ride, swim, to row and to skate, etc. Bring up a girl to be active about the house."[9] Though deaf-blind, Laura Bridgman was very active and took walks of six miles.[10]

In 1840 the school was moved from the Perkins mansion to South Boston. There were several advantages in this change, including some for physical education. Connected with the boys' school was a gymnasium which provided a bowling alley. Twice each day the boys went through exercises on the usual gymnastic fixtures to develop the muscular system. In warm weather Dr. Howe swam in the sea with the boys. This was the first physical education program for the blind in America and was far ahead of most of the physical education in the public schools. Most of the early physical education was organized by special societies, Turnvereine, etc.

In 1844 the first class for the blind in anatomy and physiology as applied to health was organized. Howe wrote: "No one subject can surpass it in importance. A sound mind cannot exist in an unsound body."[11] Six years later, a similar course was introduced in the Philadelphia school.[12]

Between 1850 and 1860 there was a general revival of physical culture in the United States. Many publications on physical education for males and females made their appearance. Baseball was beginning to develop, and the German-American Turners were

---

8. *Perkins Report*, 1841. P. 7.

9. *Ibid*, p. 8.

10. *Perkins Report*, 1842. P. 23.

11. *Perkins Report*, 1844. P. 11.

12. *Overbrook Report*, 1850. P. 11.*

*Pennsylvania Institution for the Blind.

organizing their gymnastic societies. Many gymnasiums were built. Two hundred associations of the YMCA were formed in the United States. However, there were a great many public elementary and secondary schools which did not provide any physical education.

The Indiana[13] and Philadelphia Schools for the Blind joined Perkins Institution in making special provisions for physical training classes. In Philadelphia a recess of ten minutes at the close of every hour was introduced.[14] This period for exercise in the open air is part of the school's program today. Gymnastics for boys was introduced in 1860,[15] and six years later, the first class in calisthenics for blind girls was formed.[16] New York, which was very progressive in other phases of education for the blind, finally provided supervised physical education in 1877.[17] Most of the western states educated the blind and deaf in the same school. Since there were more deaf pupils, the blind children received little attention. In California, for example, the blind students were not given physical education until 1896 and only sporadically after that for fifty years.

After nearly forty years of leadership in the education of the blind, Dr. Howe made this comparison of British and American schools: "The British schools tend to dwarf the mind by developing bodily strength and dexterity at the expense of intellectual development, ours to dwarf the body by over exercise of the mental faculties."[18] One hundred years have passed, and physical education still does not receive sufficient emphasis in many American schools.

THE EFFECT OF THE CIVIL WAR

After the Civil War military training displaced most gymnastic training in the public schools. Perkins Institution was the first to introduce military training for the blind. Within twelve years,

---

13. *Indiana Report*, 1862. P. 22.
14. *Overbrook Report*, 1859. P. 17.
15. *Overbrook Report*, 1860. P. 16.
16. *Overbrook Report*, 1866. P. 12.
17. *New York Institute Report*, 1877. P. 24.
18. *Perkins Report*, 1868. P. 22.

Overbrook,[19] Illinois[20] and Texas[21] had added military drill. The advantages of military drill for the blind were listed as erect carriage, neatness of appearance, habits of promptness, exactness, unanimity in action, manly gait, discipline and subordination.[22] Even today marching is part of the physical education curriculum for some blind students.

Between 1890 and 1900 some of the schools for the blind introduced the Swedish system of gymnastics, while others retained the German system. The Philadelphia School adopted the Swedish system in 1894[23] Four years later Perkins[24] and Pittsburgh[25] followed. During this period most of the public schools of New England secured teachers of Swedish gymnastics, while the German system was favored in the Central States. The first public gymnastic exhibition by blind students in America was given in 1893 at Philadelphia.[26] Today, these annual exhibitions are rather common in schools for the blind.

Only one school for the blind seems to have used Dr. Sargent's tables for height, weight and lung capacity. In 1897, after several years of exercise and measuring, the Philadelphia school reported[27] blind boys were 25 per cent below normal and blind girls 38 per cent below normal. Shortly before the Civil War, Dr. Howe[28] collected information from seven schools showing that blind students had 10 per cent less power to resist disease.

The decade before the turn of the century was a period of rapid growth for physical education in the public schools of the United States. In 1892, a study of the physical education programs of 272 leading cities revealed that 90 per cent of them were less than five years old. Nearly all the schools gave attention to both formal exercises and games. However, the supporters of supervised

19. *Overbrook Report,* 1884. P. 15.
20. *Illinois Report,* 1890. P. 13.
21. *Texas Report,* 1892. P. 9.
22. *Perkins Report,* 1880. P. 87.
23. *Overbrook Report,* 1894.
24. *Perkins Report,* 1898. P. 48.
25. *Western Pennsylvania Report,* 1898. P. 42.
26. *Overbrook Report,* 1893. P. 10.
27. *Overbrook Report,* 1897. P. 23.
28. *Perkins Report,* 1860. PP. 13-15.

play were winning many friends in the public schools. Many schools started intramural sports in the eighties. During the nineties interscholastic competition began to develop.

SIR FRANCIS CAMPBELL AND
THE PLAYGROUND MOVEMENT

One of the leaders of the playground movement was Dr. Campbell,* director of the Royal Normal College and Academy of Music for the Blind, London. The gymnasium of the Normal College was considered one of the most complete in all England. Besides the gymnasium there were skating rinks, a swimming pool built in 1883 and a large playground of sixteen acres.[29] The playground equipment included swings, tilts, rocking boats, rob-roys, giant-strides and balance beams.[30] Students were taught swimming, rowing and the latest methods of life-saving. A "Dunlop express" cycle carried twelve boys who helped to pedal behind a partially seeing leader.[31] The boys used to cycle fifty miles into the country. Prizes were given to the student who did the most walking. Hammer throwing and putting the shot were introduced. This program, with its equipment costing thousands of pounds, was part of the Normal College before 1900.

Dr. Campbell's aim was to discover and arrange suitable games and outdoor sports which would offer irresistible attractions for the blind. Campbell wrote: "The education of the blind whether literary, musical, or technical will not be crowned with practical success unless based upon a thorough system of physical education."[32]

In 1896 Dr. Campbell[33] pointed out certain advantages of the special school over the day classes which were soon to develop. He observed that the special schools were equipped and staffed for one purpose only, the education of blind children. The day classes for visually handicapped children sometimes lacked ade-

---

*Later Sir Francis Campbell. He was an American trained in an American school for the blind.
29. *Royal Normal College Report,* 1898. P. 17.
30. *Royal Normal College Report,* 1900. P. 19.
31. *Royal Normal College Report,* 1899. P. 29.
32. *Royal Normal College Report,* 1897. P. 17.
33. *Royal Normal College Report,* 1896. P. 26.

quate equipment, and due to insufficient training in special techniques, some subjects in many schools were not offered, or at least little emphasis was placed upon them. If Dr. Campbell were living today, he would have probably been aware of the fact that although physical education in public schools is improving in quality and quantity, more emphasis could be placed upon it in the interest of the blind child..

Soon after 1900 the play movement swept over the United States. A great deal of literature on the physical aspects of the education of the blind began to appear. In the literature of England, France[34] and the United States, the thoughts of Howe and Campbell have appeared in many forms. The physical education program for blind children laid down by these pioneers has been expanded somewhat, but the basic principles remain the same.

The first American schools for the blind to give special encouragement to play activities were Kentucky and Overbrook. Kentucky seems to have been the first school to adapt baseball, basketball, track and field and football for the blind.[35] The two former sports were played by intramural teams. The school began to compete with seeing boys in track and field in 1903. This is the first record of blind boys competing with seeing opponents. Starting in 1905, Kentucky developed a football team to compete with other schools. During the first season, the team won one, lost one and tied two.

The year 1906 is usually given as the beginning of the recreation movement in this country. Among schools for the blind Overbrook became a leader. Track, football, bowling and swimming were added to gymnastics and the less complex sports. To the athletic field were added swings, a merry-go-round, trolley slide and other playground equipment.[36] The first swimming pool for the blind in America was built at Overbrook in 1906.[37] In the next twenty years several gymnasiums and swimming pools were built for the blind—Pittsburgh (1908),[38] Iowa (gymnasium 1909, pool

34. VILLEY, P.: *La Pedagogie des Aveugles.* P. 25.
35. GREGORY, J. D.: *Athletic Sports for the Blind.* American Association of Instructors of the blind, 1907.
36. *Overbrook Report,* 1906. P. 18.
37. *Ibid.,* p. 17.
38. *Western Pennsylvania Report,* 1908.

1942), Illinois (gymnasium 1896, pool 1930), Massachusetts (1911), California (1915) and Batavia (1929).

The first intramural field day was held in 1906, with the winners' names inscribed on cups.[39] The running races were made possible by guide wires stretched 110 yds. This device had been originated in Scotland.[40] The runner holds in one hand a wooden handle attached by a short flexible chain to a ring on the wire. As he runs, the ring slips along and the feel and sound enable him to hold his course. A suspended netting was used to warn the runner to stop. Two wires were erected so that two blind boys could compete. The first year one boy ran 100 yds in 12 4/5 seconds.

In 1906 Mr. Edward E. Allen[41] reported that he had visited twenty schools for the blind and found but one where sufficient attention seemed to be paid to physical education. The southern and western schools were the most backward. In California[42] the program called for ten minutes of exercise in the classroom. By 1914 the boys were given half an hour of calisthenics.[43] Illinois[44] emphasized gymnastics, with some games and a little dancing. The senior boys entered the National Athletic Association of Schools for the Blind (NAASB) track meet. Formal exercises were stressed in Pittsburgh[45] and the New York Institute.[46] Since 1900, many of the schools for the blind have been much more formal than public schools.

In the early part of the nineteenth century Klein had adapted chess and checkers for the blind students in Vienna. These traditional games had been introduced into American schools for the blind by 1885.[47] In 1909 Perkins opened a game room with checkers, chess, bagatelle, parchesi and dominoes.[48]

The first track meet between two schools for the blind was held in 1907. The contest was a telegraphic meet between Overbrook

---

39. *Overbrook Report,* 1906. P. 13.
40. *Ibid.,* p. 13.
41. *Ibid.,* p. 12.
42. *California Report,* 1910. P. 10.
43. *California Report,* 1914. P. 10.
44. *Illinois Report,* 1914. P. 12.
45. *Western Pennsylvania Report,* 1913. P. 50.
46. *New York Institute Report,* 1906. P. 23.
47. *Overbrook Report,* 1885. P. 34.
48. *Perkins Report,* 1909. P. 15.

and the Baltimore school. A longer period of training enabled Overbrook to win all but one event.[49]

The National Athletic Association of Schools for the Blind was organized in 1908. Through the impetus furnished by the Ohio school, a committee representing the Ohio, Kentucky and Pennsylvania schools formulated a constitution and by-laws, together with a list of events and rules to govern these events.[50] The averages from large numbers of pupils were more important in the scoring than individual performances. However, one point was awarded to the individual winner of each event. This annual meet was a very important source of motivation for blind girls and boys until the Association disbanded in 1953. Results from six to fifteen schools for the blind were mailed to a central committee for comparison. Michael Goldberg served as Secretary for many, many years. Illinois won the first meet. Following are the results for the first three years.

1908		*1909*		*1910*	
Ill.	30	Ky.	38	Ky.	29
E. Pa.	13	W. Pa.	12	E. Pa.	20
Ky.	12	Ohio	11	Ohio	19
N.Y.	12	E. Pa.	10	N.Y.	19
Ohio	10	N.Y.	8	N.M.	8
W. Pa.	6	Md.	5	Mass.	5
Iowa	5	Mass.	3	W. Pa.	3
Wis.	1	Ill.	1	Ill.	1
				Montana	1
				S.C.	0
				Mo.	0

The best records of individual students in 1908 were:

12 lb shot put	35 ft 7½ in
Standing broad jump	9 ft 6 3/4 in
Standing high jump	4 ft 5½ in
50 yd dash	5.8 sec
75 yd dash	8.4 sec
Football throw	113 ft 8 in
50 yd 3-legged race	9.2 sec
50 yd sack race	10.4 sec

49. *Overbrook Report,* 1907. P. 23.
50. *Overbrook Report,* 1908. P. 16.

The first quadrangular track meet for blind athletes was held at Overbrook in 1910.[51] Overbrook won the meet, with Batavia, Perkins and Pittsburgh finishing in order. Expenses were raised by pupils of the four schools. This was a hardship, so the event did not become an annual affair.

The first Boy Scout troop for the blind was organized in Kentucky.[52] Dan Beard, who was for many years the chief of the Boy Scouts of America, visited the troop in 1911. Scout troops were organized at Overbrook in 1912 and Pittsburgh a year later. The Boy Scout and Campfire Girl movements spread rapidly to many schools for the blind. Thus, impetus was given to the movement which directed play to higher social ends.

INTERSCHOLASTIC COMPETITION WITH SEEING ATHLETES

Kentucky had competed with seeing opponents for several years by 1912. It was in this year that Overbrook,[53] Pittsburgh[54] and Perkins[55] competed with public schools for the first time. This competition was in the track and field events which offered the blind no handicap. Until 1931 interscholastic competition was very sporadic in schools for the blind except Michigan. Though this school was not the first to develop teams of blind athletes, it became the leader in this respect after 1913.[56] Michigan has developed many more athletic teams than any other school for the blind. Teams have been trained nearly every year in at least one sport—usually two or three. Michigan was the first school for the blind to introduce interscholastic competition for girls. In 1915 a basketball team of partially seeing girls represented the school. Girls' basketball teams were produced in Michigan more or less regularly until about 1950 when the sport was dropped.

It has never been an easy task to obtain equipment and train blind athletes. Pioneers in any field usually face many challenging

---

51. *Overbrook Report,* 1910. P. 22.
52. *Kentucky Report,* 1911. P. 20.
53. *Overbrook Report,* 1912. P. 60.
54. *Western Pennsylvania Report,* 1912. P. 40.
55. *Perkins Report,* 1912. P. 19 .
56. Early history of Michigan athletics was gained by correspondence from three members of the first football team—Melvin Haslip, Floyd and LeRoy Rothwell.

problems. About 1912, the Michigan School for the Blind secured the services of a vocational teacher who was intensely interested in boys. Every minute Raymond Warren had outside of the shop was spent in organizing the Boy Scouts and various athletic teams. Michigan State College and the city high schools contributed second-hand football equipment. The football team of 1913 was a motley squad with pants that came to the ankles, shoulder pads often sunk to the elbows and sweaters of all colors.. The boys were taught to play the game close to the ground. Part of the practice consisted of charging under a saw-horse and diving on the stomach when tackling. Playing a hard-hitting game close to the ground resulted in very few injuries to the players. On offense totally blind boys played center, guards and tackles. Partially seeing boys manned the other positions. The attack consisted of straight power plays through the line and around the end. On defense the totally blind boys were replaced as much as possible by partially seeing boys. Still, the boys had some difficulty tackling the opposing ball carrier and had to run up a high score to win. Michigan won about one third of the games played. The sport was discontinued about 1951.

In 1915 an athletic association of boys and girls was formed. The association made money selling candy, salvaging waste paper and using every means available to give financial aid to athletics in general. At times, $300 or $400 was available for athletic equipment. This helped the spirit of the teams a great deal. The boys and girls became more willing to make a strong effort in athletics. Through the years the blind students of Michigan have made many sacrifices to compete with small local schools. A fine spirit of sportsmanship has grown up. The University of Notre Dame is not the only school willing to put the "it" into athletics. It might be said also that these students have received a great deal from athletic training. Warren's early efforts have been rewarded, because today Michigan probably provides more athletic equipment for its blind students than any other state.

Wrestling, which has become the most popular interscholastic sport for the blind, was introduced at the New York State School[57]

57. Information obtained from Thomas Beadnell, a former student.

as early as 1902. The competition was intramural and did not become interscholastic in this school until 1940. Pittsburgh was the first school for the blind to discover the value of competing with seeing opponents in wrestling.[58] Early in 1916 a wrestling room was equipped. Chester Smith, a member of the University of Pittsburgh wrestling team, became coach. Interest ran high among the boys. In 1917 the wrestling team won all but two matches with various clubs in the city. There were no high school wrestling teams in Pittsburgh at that time. The war interrupted the program, but it was resumed in the fall of 1919. The team completed two seasons undefeated, wrestling YMCA and Bureau of Recreation teams. Several of the blind boys won city championships. Harry Auen won the 135 lb Middle Atlantic AAU championship. The sport was discontinued after 1921 because Coach Smith became a teacher in the Pittsburgh public schools.[59]

Another outstanding collegiate wrestler, Neal Quimby, introduced wrestling at Overbrook about ten years later. Overbrook gave the real impetus to wrestling by the blind. Soon Baltimore, New York Institute, Perkins, West Virginia, Washington, Oregon and a few other schools began to develop wrestling teams to compete with other schools for the blind and seeing high school opponents. Overbrook lost no meets between 1933 and 1938. The team defeated the freshman team of the University of Pennsylvania and all the outstanding local high schools in Philadelphia. In 1939 Overbrook suffered its only defeat at the hands of the New York Institute for the Blind.

One member of the Overbrook team later (1939) became captain of the varsity wrestling team at the University of Pennsylvania.

The movement into the country has had its influence upon the physical education of the blind. Within a period of ten years, three large eastern schools moved to the suburbs—Overbrook, 1904, Baltimore, 1911, and Perkins, 1914. Many schools already had rural or semirural sites—California, Oregon, Washington, Arizona, New Mexico, Utah, Oklahoma, Iowa, Illinois, Wisconsin, Minnesota, South Carolina, etc. In 1915 Perkins established the

---

58. *Western Pennsylvania Report,* 1917. P. 44.
59. Information obtained by correspondence with Chester Smith.

first summer camp for blind children. New York Institute and a few other schools have made provisions for summer camping.

Shortly after 1920 the first nurseries for blind infants were founded. These institutions recognize the basic importance of physical education for the blind. Diet, proper clothing, fresh air and directed play help to make blind infants physically normal. Some parents have learned the proper care for rearing healthy blind children. As more parents of blind children become aware of the objective approach, there will be much more progress in physical education in public and residential schools. The schools, starting with better material, will not have to use valuable time to correct mistakes made in the past.

It was not until after 1920 that most of the southern and western schools for the blind had accepted the play movement. The connection with the deaf had been a hindering factor. In California the two schools were separated to their reciprocal advantage in 1921. One of the results for the blind was the introduction of a fine program of games and dancing by Vivien Osborn. She wrote the first master's thesis[60] on the physical education of the blind. The most valuable material in Osborn's thesis was made available to schools for the blind in the *Outlook for the Blind* in 1926.

After having been used in England for a number of years, eurhythmics were introduced into the New York and Philadelpha schools for the blind. Several advantages were claimed for this activity, but it never became very widely used.

Through the years practically every school for the blind has given some attention to corrective gymnastics. Due to the large number of students and the limited time of the instructor, corrective work has never been entirely successful. Often the teacher does not possess the necessary training in corrective exercises. In 1934[61] Perkins took a long step toward solving this problem. An arrangement was made to have physiotherapists from the Harvard Medical School give treatments to students at the school for the blind. Of course, not all schools are so fortunate to be located near a large university.

---

60. OSBORN, V.: *Physical Education for Blind Girls.* Master's thesis, University of California, 1927.
61. *Perkins Report,* 1934. P. 53.

In 1938 buzzer baseball[62] for the blind was introduced on the West coast.[63] The base paths are wooden footways three feet in width, and the bases are wired with electrical buzzers which are operated by the umpire. This variation of the American game has found more favor with blind adults than children. The Ohio school is one of the very few that has introduced it to blind children. Buzzer baseball, like all modifications, is far from being an entirely satisfactory adaptation.

A HISTORIC DECADE

During the decade 1940-1950 World War II was fought, and our nation's strength was taxed to the utmost. At the same time, a number of developments were taking place in physical education of blind children that have influenced today's program. It was during this time that Neal Quimby[64] and a few others made suggestions as to what might be taught in the physical education program that would be carried over into the years beyond graduation. The physical activities most likely to be engaged in by blind adults are hiking, bowling, swimming, rowing, camping, roller skating, ice skating, wrestling and dancing. More schools are giving more emphasis to these activities.

Most of the schools for the blind have organized clubs which combine instruction and play. One serious disadvantage of many of these clubs is that they do not have contacts with children who have normal vision. Some of the more common groups are Boy Scouts, Girl Scouts, Cub Scouts, dramatic clubs, girls' and boys' athletic associations, music clubs, etc.

The exceptional success of blind chess players in the British championship tournaments has called attention to the importance of the game in the life of blind individuals. Worcester College for the Blind in England organized a chess club as early as 1934.[65] During World War II and a few years afterward, the California

---

62. *Recreation,* February, 1939.
63. *Pic Magazine,* Vol. *8:* No. 7, 1940, pp. 40-41.
64. QUIMBY, N. F.: What Activities That May be Taught in a Physical Education Program May be an Incentive for Leisure-Ttime Activities, *AAIB Proceedings,* 1940, pp. 133-135.
65. BROWN, G. C.: Worcester College for the Blind Chess Club, *New Beacon, 18:* 1934, p. 287.

School for the Blind[66] chess team won most of its matches with local high schools and competed on equal terms with adult chess clubs in the area.

It was normal that World War II should draw attention to physical fitness. In 1944, the author[67] introduced the Navy Testing Program at the Michigan School for the Blind. A few years later Buell[68] extended his study to include 650 boys in twenty special schools. By 1950 his investigation[69] was broadened and extended to more students, 519 boys and 346 girls in twelve residential schools and eight Braille classes in public schools. Some of the conclusions drawn from these studies were:

1. Mean scores of visually handicapped boys and girls fall far below those of seeing students in the 50-yard dash, basketball throw and on all levels of the Iowa Brace Test:
2. Groups of blind and seeing pupils complete on about equal terms in sit-ups, pull-ups and the standing broad jump:
3. The partially seeing excel the blind in running and throwing, but the groups compete on a more equal basis in the standing broad jump:
4. Overprotected blind and partially seeing children score below normal in track and field events and the Iowa Brace Test: and
5. Children who lose their vision after six years of age perform better in track and field events than do those blind from birth.

Buell's studies are the basis of achievement and physical fitness testing today. This subject will be discussed in more detail in a later chapter.

SUMMARY

Some of the schools for the blind have been quick to grasp new ideas in physical education and adapt them, if necessary. One

66. RICKARD, R.: Chess and checkers for the blind, *Outlook for the Blind*, May, 1946, pp. 121-124.
67. BUELL, CHARLES: Physical fitness testing in a school for the blind. *Outlook for the Blind*, December, 1945, pp. 280-282.
68. BUELL, CHARLES: The Navy Testing Program in schools for the blind. *Outlook for the Blind*, March, 1947, pp. 78-79.
69. BUELL, CHARLES: *Motor Performance of Visually Handicapped Children.* Ann Arbor, Michigan, Edwards Brothers, 1950, 125 pp.

might expect that more games and devices should have been developed for special use of the visually handicapped. The prevailing thought has been to adapt the public school program rather than invent something that might be of even more value to sightless individuals. During the first hundred years of education of the blind in the United States, gymnastics and marching received undue attention. Until World War II, educators experienced much difficulty in securing adequate athletic equipment. This was due to the limited number of blind children in each state and the lack of recognition of the importance of physical education for the visually handicapped on the part of some educators. During this period, many of the western and southern schools were ten to twenty years behind the leaders in physical education of blind pupils.

Through the years, there have been two opposing views of physical education, the *compulsory-formal* theory and the *play* theory. The formal system of physical education develops strong muscles and the latter develops certain mental qualities, such as fighting spirit and teamwork. Before the first World War most schools based their programs on the *compulsory-formal* theory, stressing toughening up for the next war. By 1920 most educators were convinced that games were more valuable than formal exercises. The *play* theory was dominant for twenty years. World War II proved that games do not develop the physical condition necessary for war. As a result, physical educators came to the conclusion that their objectives could be best attained by combining the two theories, using calisthenics and games. The strong points of one theory are the weak points of the other; the programs supplement each other. Schools for the blind have adopted this combined system because the principles underlying their work do not differ essentially from those that guide work in the regular program of physical education.

Chapter 3

DEVELOPMENTS IN PHYSICAL EDUCATION FOR BLIND CHILDREN IN MODERN TIMES

IN THE LAST TWENTY YEARS there has been a rapid growth in the belief that a blind child is an integral part of the community. The feeling has grown that the community has an obligation to provide an education for all of its children, including those who are blind. Local school districts have the same obligation to provide a suitable education for the retarded and emotionally disturbed blind child as they have for the retarded and emotionally disturbed seeing child.

Due to the change in the philosophy of the education of blind children, many more visually handicapped pupils are being placed in schools in their home communities. At the end of World War II, about 10 per cent of all blind children were attending public schools. Today, more than 60 per cent of all blind pupils are being educated in community schools, rather than in residential schools for the blind. This change in placement of a large segment of these children has resulted in marked changes in the educational program for them. Here we are interested in the aspects of physical education and recreation. Some public schools have accepted their responsibility to provide physical education for all children, including those who are blind. Unfortunately, some of these programs are so modified that they do not develop the physical fitness required by visually handicapped individuals. Many blind boys and girls in the public schools are not given any physical education. It is feasible for blind children to take physical education with their seeing classmates in the public schools. Fortunately, such programs are being organized in more and more communities. With improved understanding of the physical abilities of blind individuals and the realization that sightless persons do not have any more accidents than do children who have normal vision, physical education for blind children is spreading in public schools. Another result of the change in philosophy has been a rapid increase in participation of blind girls and boys in family and community recreational activities.

A result of World War II was the introduction into the Maryland School for the Blind of foot travel by Richard Hoover in 1946. He had developed the basic physical education program for returning blinded veterans at Valley Forge General Hospital. Foot travel enables a blind individual to walk freely. A lightweight cane is held protectively aslant the body or moved back and forth lightly, touching the ground in front of the foot which is about to be brought forward. This training is now offered to older pupils in most schools and some classes in public schools as a course in orientation and mobility.

The introduction of training in travel techniques had a definite influence on the physical education program. Educators became more aware that a boy or girl who is physically fit and alert travels faster, farther, more accurately and more safely. Therefore, good programs of physical education are basic to the success of the orientation and mobility program.

Early in 1947 nine schools organized the Eastern Athletic Association for the Blind. Maryland's Joseph Lyons and William Shellnut of Overbrook were largely responsible for starting the association, which has held annual wrestling tournaments and track meets for twenty years. Since this was face-to-face competition it was only a matter of time until the National Athletic Association of Schools for the Blind was forced to discontinue its mail-o-graphic competition.

The first wrestling tournament[1] was held at Johns Hopkins University in Baltimore, March 14 and 15, 1947. The tourney was strongly contested by fifty boys from six schools. Team scores were:

Overbrook	37
Maryland	24
Virginia	22
W. Virginia	16
Perkins	14
Kentucky	3

---

1. Information obtained by correspondence from Joseph Lyons, who was formerly a teacher at the Maryland School for the Blind.

Hugh Arnold of the Maryland School for the Blind won the 133 lb title. He has served as boys' physical education teacher in Baltimore many years now. Fegley of Overbrook was the outstanding wrestler. Joseph Kerr was the Secretary and has served the EAAB in this capacity for eighteen years.

The first track meet of the Eastern Athletic Association of the Blind was held in Philadelphia on May 17, 1947.[2] Flowers of Overbrook won the dashes, while Fenwick of Virginia excelled in the jumping events. Teams scored in the following order:

Virginia	25½
Overbrook	22½
New York Institute	11
Maryland	10
Kentucky	4
Batavia, N.Y.	2
Perkins	2
W. Virginia	0
Connecticut	0

RECENT DEVELOPMENTS

The Eastern Athletic Association of the Blind set the pattern for the formation of other similar associations. In 1951 the Midwestern Athletic Association of the Blind was formed and held its first wrestling tournament. Team scores were:

Iowa	38
Arkansas	30
Oklahoma	23
Wisconsin	17
Kansas	10
Kentucky	9
Missouri	3

In the early tournaments Leonard Ogburn was outstanding in both wrestling and track and field. For the past several years he has been a successful coach of blind boys in Alabama and Virginia.

Due to the number of schools involved it was decided in the spring of 1956 to split the Midwestern Association into two organizations. It was a severe hardship on the host residential school to

---

2. Information obtained from Joseph Kerr, Overbrook School for the Blind, Philadelphia, Pennsylvania.

supply sufficient housing for the large number of competitors entering the annual wrestling tournament. Another factor was the long travel distances for some schools. The solution was very temporary because these problems soon returned to haunt administrators and athletic directors. Charter members of the North Central Association were Missouri, Kansas, Kentucky, Illinois, Iowa, Nebraska, Minnesota and South Dakota. In recent years Michigan, Wisconsin, Indiana and Ohio have been added to again make the Association uncomfortably large. The Southwestern Athletic Association of Schools for the Blind has as members Texas, Arkansas, New Mexico, Tennessee, Oklahoma and Colorado. It is evident that long travel distances have been a stumbling block for this Association. Another difficulty is that a great variation exists in the size of enrollments of member schools, tending to make competition uneven. For these and other reasons, the Association has been gradually disintegrating. This is most unfortunate because some of the country's finest blind athletes have come from schools in the Southwest.

In 1958, the Southeastern Association of Schools for the Blind was organized for competition in track and field for girls and boys.[3] Since more and more of these schools are taking up wrestling, this sport may be added to the competition soon. The members of the Association are Alabama, Florida, Georgia, Mississippi, Louisiana and Tennessee. Perhaps the most noteworthy feature of this organization is that competition for girls was inaugurated. Interscholastic competition for girls has been sponsored recently by some schools of the Eastern Association, and it is hoped the movement will spread to other sections of the country. Carol Wadell of Perkins is a leading force in the movement.

Of course, play days have long been a part of the intramural program of many schools for the blind. After World War II, play days for girls were extended to include other schools for the blind and, in some cases, public schools. Twenty-five to fifty blind girls participate in annual play days held in the East, Midwest and Southwest.

Western schools for the blind have been organized for competition in a decathlon for boys and a similar event for girls. The

---

3. See Appendix E.

girls compete in the fall, while the boys' events are held in the spring. Buell's achievement scales[4] are used for both decathlons. In some ways the organization is similar to the disbanded National Athletic Association of Schools for the Blind. All pupils over ten years of age are expected to participate with the hope that motivation will be widespread. School averages are most important in the scoring, but awards are made to the top ten individuals in each division. Since one event a week is held, at least ten weeks are required to complete the decathlon. Much sustained interest has been aroused in the participating schools. Each year approximately 250 students participate in this mail-o-graphic competition. (See Appendix F.)

In the Southwest, New Mexico and Texas have been the leaders in wrestling, while Texas and Arkansas have excelled in track and field. (See Appendices B and C.)

In the Midwest, Missouri, Michigan and Kansas have been the leaders in wrestling, and Missouri has dominated the track and field competition. (See Appendix D.)

The Eastern leaders in wrestling have been Virginia and Overbrook, while Virginia and Maryland have excelled in track and field. (See Appendix A.) One of the most unusual and outstanding performances in track and field took place at the Eastern Association Track Meet in 1955. A single athlete scored all of the points as Batavia, New York, won the championship. This one-man track team won four first places to score 20 points, while the best Virginia, in second place, could do was to gain 15 points. The most familiar figure at tournaments and track meets of the Eastern Association was Dr. Francis Andrews, who was a leader in the organization until his retirement as Superintendent of the Maryland School for the Blind in 1965.

In 1960 a national committee[5] was formed to standardize track and field rules for blind athletes in all parts of the United States. Under the leadership of Charles R. Young of Texas a great deal has been accomplished, including the evaluation and acceptance of national records[6] for visually handicapped boys.

---

4. See Chapter 12.

5. *Proceedings, American Association of Instructors of the Blind,* 1960. p. 84.

6. See page 84.

After 1950 interest in the sport of bowling began to grow in schools for the blind. Teams from California, Washington and Tennessee began competing in leagues and tournaments sponsored by the American Junior Bowling Congress. Under the leadership of V. R. Carter, Superintendent of the Oklahoma School for the Blind, the National Bowling League of Schools for the Blind was formed in the fall of 1958. Sixteen schools participated in the first season's competition, and the number of teams has remained fairly constant each season. The mail-o-graphic competition is divided into three divisions, Open, Girls and Juniors. California, Georgia, Missouri and Nebraska have entered teams in all three divisions, while a number of schools enter teams in two divisions. Participating schools in 1965 were Ohio, Overbrook, Missouri, Alabama, Michigan, Oklahoma, Kansas, Nebraska, South Dakota, Jericho Hill (Canada), Washington, Oregon, California, Idaho and Georgia. League competition involves thirty teams and over 165 bowlers. Some schools which are not in the league, such as Perkins, Maryland, Arizona, New Mexico, Iowa and Tennessee, have nevertheless greatly enlarged their programs of bowling. This increased emphasis on bowling is highly desirable because it is one of the few carry-over activities of the physical education program into home and adult life.

In the 1962 Mail-o-graphic Handicap Tournament of the American Junior Bowling Congress, a team from the California School for the Blind placed sixth in California and eighty-third nationally in a field of 2,300 teams in the Senior Boys Division. This is the only time a team of blind bowlers has placed in the top one hundred teams of the tournament.

In 1956 six boys from the Arizona School for the Blind hiked 21 miles from Hopi Point over some of the most tortuous trails in North America to Bright Angel Point on the North Rim. These boys mastered the Grand Canyon in twelve hours. The trip was repeated for about four years with Charles Thornton as the sighted guide.

In the last fifteen years there has been a marked increase in the emphasis placed on activities that aid orientation of blind children.[7] Metronomes, audible balls, bells, speakers in the corners of gym-

---

7. *Proceedings, American Association of Instructors of the Blind,* 1962. pp. 131-132.

nasiums, audible basketball locators and other sounds are now used much more frequently in physical education classes for visually handicapped boys and girls. Contests which aid orientation were introduced and include such problems as walking as close to a wall as possible without touching it. Perkins, California and some other schools added asphalt base paths to their baseball diamonds. Students first learn to walk and then run on them.

A marked increase in the use of the trampoline by blind children took place after World War II. The rebound tumbling program of the Washington State School for the Blind received national attention when a trampoline company launched an advertising program in many sport and physical education journals. Two-page articles told the story of blind children using the trampoline. Rebound tumbling not only provides a rich store for teaching basic body movements, but it can do much in developing orientation skills.

During the past decade some schools for the blind, such as California, Oregon, Washington, Missouri and Nebraska, have placed much more emphasis on outdoor education. In some schools the program has become a part of the curriculum[8] and is no longer limited to summer camp experiences or boy and girl scout activities. These programs emphasize hiking, fishing, conservation, nature study, outdoor cooking, working together and recreational aquatics. Each year large numbers of pupils at the Washington State School for the Blind plant trees in rough terrain which was devastated by a large forest fire years ago.

In a number of states, schools for the blind have been pioneers in interscholastic wrestling. Some of these states are California, Texas, Arkansas, Alabama, Florida, Tennessee, Missouri, Nebraska and New Mexico. In 1961 the Kentucky School for the Blind sponsored the first wrestling tournament of high schools in the state.

Many blind individuals have compiled outstanding records in wrestling, but the most outstanding team effort has come from the Michigan School for the Blind, which won the State Class B wrestling title in 1961 and 1963. Class B schools in Michigan in-

---

8. WOODCOCK, C. C.: School Camping in Oregon. *New Outlook for the Blind,* June, 1956. See also HALLIDAY, C.: School Camping—A Meaningful Experience. *New Outlook for the Blind,* March, 1964.

clude enrollments up to 900. Lloyd Frees won eighty-five wrestling bouts and lost only four during his high school competition to lead the team. He received national recognition when he won third place on the 1964 Honor Roll of High School Wrestlers of the Amateur Wrestling News.

FIGURE 2. State High School Wrestling Champions 1963, Class B, Michigan School for the Blind.

In January, 1961, Dr. Neal F. Quimby, Superintendent of the New Mexico School for the Visually Handicapped, passed away. Thirty-two years before his untimely death he introduced interscholastic wrestling into schools for the blind. He saw his experiment blossom into "the sport" for 75 per cent of the schools for the blind. Wrestling has made it possible for a blind boy to compete against opponents with normal vision on equal terms. It is impossible to estimate the amount of confidence wrestling has developed in blind boys, together with perserverance, pride of achievement, physical fitness, sportmanship and the other fine qualities of this sport. Dr. Quimby's pioneer efforts, his excellent coaching record, his zeal in spirit in teaching sportsmanship and the high opinion of all those who associated with him are qualities that led the Helms Amateur Wrestling Hall of Fame to select him as a member. Thus, national attention was drawn to wrestling for blind boys.

When Michael Goldberg retired in 1957 he had served as physical education teacher and scout master at the New York State School for the Blind in Batavia for forty-one years. He was a devoted, faithful worker who believed firmly in the abilities of the visually handicapped. He gave student demonstrations all over western New York State and in many other ways "sold" the public on the abilities of blind individuals. Michael Goldberg adapted many games for the use of visually handicapped children. For over thirty years he was Secretary and President of the National Athletic Association of Schools for the Blind. His long service was filled with many highlights of accomplishment, but the true measure of the man lay in his constant, daily interest in the welfare of his students.

Another outstanding physical educator who recently retired was William Burrows of Virginia. Inez Holmes has faithfully served the Wisconsin School for the Visually Handicapped as girls' physical education teacher for over thirty years.

Within the last twelve years general improvements have been made in physical education for blind children. About one half of the residential schools have made major additions in the form of gymnasiums, swimming pools and bowling lanes. Within the past six years residential schools in New York City, Philadelphia, Boston, Wisconsin, Minnesota, Iowa, Kansas, Alabama, Michigan, Illinois, Nebraska and Washington State have opened new gymnasiums, most of them with bowling lanes and some of them with swimming pools. Overbrook's field house was built at a cost of three quarters of a million dollars, and the other structures will adequately meet needs for many years. Schools for the blind in Arizona, Texas and Indiana have recently opened new swimming pools. Not long ago blind boys and girls in Idaho moved into a remodeled gymnasium which more adequately met their needs. Seven years ago students of the California School for the Blind took possession of a large gymnasium and later a swimming pool and bowling lane, formerly shared with deaf boys and girls. In the last twelve years gymnasiums have been completed in Ohio.

Florida, Maryland, Virginia, West Virginia, Oregon, Arizona and New Mexico.

During this time schools for the blind have added to their personnel in the areas of physical education and recreation. Full-time recreation directors are now employed in Texas, Missouri, Connecticut, North Carolina, Illinois, Nebraska and Michigan.

SUMMARY

Since World War II the percentage of blind children attending public schools has increased sixfold. So far many of these children are not receiving adequate physical education. However, more and more such programs are being organized.

The residential schools have gone through a period of rapid expansion in such facilities as gymnasiums, bowling lanes and pools. The addition of these facilities has greatly stimulated and expanded the physical education programs in these schools. Due to better communication and better travel conditions, interscholastic competition has markedly increased among schools for the blind. The increased visitation of teachers among the schools has been very beneficial in spreading new ideas.

One task is far from completed. This is the dissemination of factual information on all aspects of blindness. As the needs and abilities of the visually handicapped become known to parents, teachers and the general public, the education and welfare of this minority group will improve. Athletics has played an important role in educating the public, and it is expected to be a leading force in the future.

Chapter 4

PHYSICAL EDUCATION FOR VISUALLY HANDICAPPED CHILDREN IN PUBLIC SCHOOLS

GUIDING PRINCIPLES

IT IS THE RESPONSIBILITY of the school to contribute to the fullest possible development of the potentialities of each individual entrusted to its care. This is a basic tenet of our democratic faith. In the words of Dr. Berthold Lowenfeld: "The community has an obligation to provide for the education of its children—all of its children—wherever this appears feasible." Since educating blind children in all respects, physical and mental, is feasible, local public schools should maintain and increase their facilities and educational services for blind children.

Today, over 60 per cent of visually handicapped children are attending public schools. More and more communities are accepting the responsibility of preparing these children to become well-adjusted, contributing members of society. Unfortunately, many of these communities are not extending every educational opportunity to their blind children. A conservative estimate is that at least two-thirds of the blind pupils attending public schools are not given any physical education, while some of the others are offered a program which has very little value. Some public schools have clearly demonstrated that a vigorous program of physical education is feasible for visually handicapped boys and girls. All schools which have blind students should include them in the physical education curriculum. Ways in which this can be done will be discussed below.

Sometimes special methods are used in physical education of blind children, just as special methods are used in academic instruction. These are used only when they offer the best way to attain the goal.

The program of physical activities should be carefully regulated to meet the individual's special needs. The aim is to develop as much physical fitness, along with the other desirable qualities, as the student's medical condition will safely permit. Most children can safely participate in many of the activities of the regular physical education class. Some blind boys and girls, as well as seeing children, have medical conditions which should somewhat limit physical activity. However, there is hardly a blind student who should not participate in some type of physical education. Of course, competent and intelligent leadership must be provided.

A thorough physical examination should be given by a physician before participation in physical education is permitted. Adequate health examinations should be repeated at periodic intervals or whenever observation indicates that the service may be needed. However, physicians and opthal-mologists have a responsibility to inform themselves concerning the goals and the program of physical education for visually handicapped children. An informed physician will encourage the blind youngster to participate fully in physical education, except in the few cases where physical conditions will not permit. Every student in school should participate daily in an activity suitable for him.

Sometimes conditions of visual impairment exist which could result in further damage and loss of vision, if unrestricted activities such as wrestling and football were permitted. Some students who are high myopes should not participate in contact and rough sports because of the possibility of detaching the retina. However, activities can be selected which are safe for them and will make a valuable contribution to their welfare.

Adapted physical education is growing rapidly. More and more colleges are giving instruction in the subject to their candidates for teaching physical education. Some states now require that all physical education teachers have instruction in adapted physical education. The number of magazine articles, books [1], and[2] films[3]

1. FAIT, HOLLIS: *Adapted Physical Education.* Philadelphia, W. B. Saunders, 1960, 332 pp.
2. DANIELS, A. S., and DAVIES, E. A.: *Adapted Physical Education: Principles and Practice of Physical Education for Exceptional Students.* New York, Harper and Row, 1965, 547 pp.
3. Charles Buell, California School for the Blind, 3001 Derby St., Berkeley, Calif. 94705.

appearing on the subject is increasing. Still, many schools do not yet have teachers trained in adapted physical education. Many other schools, particularly on the elementary level, do not have trained teachers in regular physical education.

In California the state makes available to school districts additional funds to organize programs for handicapped children, including those with visual impairments. Some funds may perhaps be available in other states, or additional money might be provided for the purpose by individual school districts.

TWO BASIC CONSIDERATIONS

Perhaps the most common reason given or implied for not offering physical education to blind children in the public schools is the fear of injury. Some administrators feel that an injury to a sightless child is of more consequence than it is for other children. Those who have had experience of any length with handicapped individuals will testify that this is not true. Many school administrators assume that visually handicapped youngsters are more prone to accidents. Long ago residential schools for the blind discovered that they did not have any more accidents than did the neighboring public schools attended by seeing children. Furthermore, the public schools which have given physical education to all students have found that injuries are no more common or severe among blind youngsters than among the rest of the student body.

Another reason commonly given for not including blind children in physical education in the public schools is that it would require more supervision on the part of the teacher who already has all he can handle. Teachers in such circumstances can solve the problem by pairing the blind child with a classmate who has normal vision. In almost every class the teacher will find a student who is willing and capable of giving his visually handicapped classmate the assistance he needs. By doing this little or no additional supervision is required on the part of the teacher.

SHOULD A BLIND CHILD BE PLACED IN AN ADAPTED CLASS?

Since elementary schools usually do not offer adapted physical education, the problem will arise in those secondary schools which offer such a program. The answer to the question will depend upon the individual and the environment. A junior or senior high school boy or girl who has a physical irregularity, such as a weak heart or those few eye conditions which might be aggravated by regular activities, should be placed in a class for adapted physical education. It is likely that a blind child who has poor mobility may gain more from adapted activities. On the other hand, a very athletic blind boy or girl may benefit more from participation in the regular class. It will depend upon where the visually handicapped youngster can attain most of his goals in physical education, the most important being vigorous physical fitness to meet the extra demands made upon him in daily living. However, the development of mobility, control of body and sports skills should not be overlooked. In some schools more blind children attain these goals in the adapted class, while in others they are better attained in the regular physical education program.

One plan that has proved very successful on the secondary level is to place the blind student according to units of instruction, rather than assign him to a class. For example, a blind boy might be placed in units on wrestling, weight training, tumbling, rebound tumbling, gymnastics and swimming rather than softball, basketball, flag football or volleyball. This means that during the school year a blind student may become a member of a number of classes for a limited time. He is assigned to those activities which will contribute the most toward his welfare.

Perhaps mention should be made here of the importance of the teacher explaining to the rest of the class the needs, desires and abilities of their blind classmate. This understanding, which is so necessary to the success of the handicapped individual, will not develop without intelligent planning. Of course, this means that the teacher must obtain accurate information beforehand.

ACTIVITIES

There are a number of activities which require little or no modification for use by blind boys and girls. Some of them are wrestling, gymnastics, rebound tumbling, tumbling, swimming, many relays, races, some track and field events, dancing and rhythms, hiking, bowling, many individual combatives, rope climbing, tug-of-war, push ball, pull-ups, sit-ups, squat-thrusts, calisthenics, rope jumping, trainer bicycling, rowing, weight training, singing games, tag games and other low organizational activities. Physical fitness testing and motivation can be carried on by using Buell's adaptation of some of the AAHPER Scales. (See Chapter 12.) For information on desirable modifications of activities, refer to Chapters 7, 8 and 9.

WAYS IN WHICH BLIND CHILDREN COME TO THE ATTENTION OF PUBLIC SCHOOL TEACHERS

Visually handicapped children come to the attention of teachers in public schools in at least three distinct situations: (a) classroom teachers with an occasional blind or partially seeing child; (b) physical educators with an occasional visually handicapped child; and (c) teacher of classes for the blind or partially seeing for which no leadership in physical education is available. Just because an activity is listed here under one heading, it need not be limited to that particular group.

Classroom Teachers with an Occasional Blind or Partially Seeing Child

In most elementary schools the classroom teachers are required to conduct physical education for their students. This can be a real problem for a teacher who is not familiar with the subject. By referring to Chapter 13, most information can be gained concerning recommended activities for different grade levels and the amount of time that should be spent on each. A limited number of suitable activities will be discussed in more detail below, showing how an occasional blind child fits into the picture.

The singing games and imitation activities which appeal so much to preschool and primary children usually need no adaptation for a visually handicapped boy or girl. In the intermediate grades, 25 per cent of physical education time is usually devoted to rhythms or dancing. In teaching a dance these factors should be considered.

1. Give the name of the dance and tell the children something about the country from which it comes.
2. Play the music. If the rhythm is difficult, have the children clap it.

3. Describe and demonstrate the first step.
4. Teach steps in slow tempo at first.
5. Teach by musical phrases rather than by count.
6. When a step has been learned, put it with the other steps to preserve the continuity of the dance.
7. Review dances often. The better known a dance is the more it is enjoyed.

In most dances the sighted children can give their blind classmate the assistance he needs. In a few dances limited variations may be helpful. Hands may be kept joined to hold a formation instead of moving them. Movements may sometimes be performed in place instead of using difficult formations.

About one third of the physical education time of elementary school children should be spent on games. When a blind child is in the class, games should be selected with more care so that he can participate on an equal basis with his seeing classmates. Of course, games in which one or two players are blindfolded come to mind. Be alert to the possibility of pairing up a blind child with a seeing partner. Games using line or chain formations are good. Where possible, use activities that feature sound. If games do not ordinarily feature sound, sighted playmates can be asked to shout or clap hands to assist the blind child in locating them. Games played in a limited area with a goal to run to that easily can be found by a sightless child are desirable. Each of the following games were selected as an example of one or more of the characteristics mentioned above.

Dodge Ball

This is a game commonly played in the intermediate grades. When a blind child is in the circle dodging the ball, he may pair up with a seeing boy or girl who will assist him. When it is the blind student's turn to attempt to hit someone with the ball, the players in the circle should clap hands or shout. Otherwise, the game is played in the usual manner.

Chain Tag

When a blind player participates in chain tag the playing area should have definite boundaries, such as fences, walls, side of buildings, edges of lawns or concrete surfaces. The players scatter over the playing area. At the signal, one player who is "it" chases the others. When he tags a runner the latter joins hands with him, and the two together chase the other players. A catch or tag made while the line is broken is invalid. The game continues until all but one have joined the chain. He is the winner and "it" for the next game. So that a sightless player may have a fair opportunity to win, he may be paired up with a classmate who has normal vision, and the two of them attempt to avoid being caught. More mobile sightless players should be encouraged to run alone. In this case the chain should be required to hold him for ten counts before he is considered caught.

Barley Break

A rectangular strip of asphalt or lawn is a good barley field. The players pair up in couples and grasp hands. One pair stands in the barley field and tries to tag couples who venture into the field, tramping down the barley and shouting "Barley break!" When two players are caught, they become the custodians of the barley field.

Japanese Torpedo

The teacher must select a torpedo which will make noise. Indoors, a small bag of sand may be covered with emery cloth, while outside, on an asphalt surface, a small metal tray or flattened tin can serves the purpose. The torpedo is attached to a long rope, and the players arrange themselves in a large circle. One player takes his place in the center of the circle and begins to swing the rope so that the torpedo slides around and around on the ground. The players jump over the rope as it passes. When a player is hit, a point is counted against him. The player with the lowest score at the end of five minutes of play is the winner. The game can be played by having the players in the circle grasp hands, or couples grasping hands.

Animal Blind Man's Buff

One player is blindfolded and takes his position in the center of the circle. The players in the circle grasp hands and dance around the blind man until he taps the floor with a broomstick.

The blind man then points his stick at a player and commands him to make a noise like a cat, dog, duck or some other animal. From this the blind man tries to guess the name of the player. If he succeeds, they exchange places. If he fails, the game is repeated with the same blind man.

Ball Wrestle

Two to six boys take a kneeling position around a basketball. Each boy starts with one hand on the ball and the other hand on his hip. When the signal "Go" is given, each boy attempts to wrest the ball from his opponents and stand up with it at full arm's length overhead. If the contest is not won in two or three minutes, it should be called a draw. While the boys rest, another group can wrestle.

Relays

One way to include a blind child in relays is to select those which are run in couples, such as Siamese relay, wheelbarrow relay, cowboy relay and couple relay.

(a) Two players stand back to back and hook elbows. They move toward the turning line, one running forward and the other backward. Upon reaching the turning line they stop and without turning around, return to the starting line. (b) One player grasps the other's ankles, and he walks on his hands. At the turning line, positions are reversed. (c) One player mounts the other's back. They reverse positions at the turning line. (d) Players run in couples, holding hands.

Physical Educators With an Occasional Visually Handicapped Child

A number of physical education activities need little or no modification for blind boys and girls. Blind boys have won varsity letters in wrestling, gymnastics, tumbling and rowing, while partially seeing boys have won similar honors in track and field and football. Weight training, swimming, dancing, calisthenics and bowling are other activities suitable for visually handicapped individuals. See Chapters 9 and 10 for suggestions on relays, races and contests.

In some activities it is advisable to make adaptations for blind

FIGURE 3. Blind tumblers—California.

players. Reference should be made to Chapter 7, but a few modifications of sports are mentioned below.

Track and Field

Such events as standing broad jump, standing triple jump, standing high jump, shot put, basketball throw for distance, pull-ups, rope climb, tug-of-war, and rope jump need no modification for the blind. In distance running a sightless student should run hand in hand with a seeing partner. In dashes, it is best if a seeing child runs 5 to 10 yds in front of a blind youngster. The seeing assistant should shout constantly or blow a whistle.

Softball

In a number of public schools, a blind player is permitted to hit the ball after it has been placed on a 3-ft-high tee. He runs to a teammate who is calling him on first base. If it is safe to run farther, the two continue around the bases as partners, grasping hands.

Football

Two modifications should be made in football to accommodate blind players. The ball should be put in play by shouting "Hike!" The ball carrier should continue to shout so that the blind defensive player can locate and tackle him. Sightless players perform well at center, guard and tackle positions.

Volleyball

The blind player should do all of the serving for his team. It may take some practice to develop acceptable skill.

Basketball Goal Ball

Players throw the basketball back and forth. The ball is thrown from the point where it is stopped, and players take turns as in a batting order. The game is played on a basketball court. For seeing players one point is awarded for hitting the backboard and three for making a basket. A sightless player should be awarded double score. When a blind player is attempting to score, a bell hanging on the backboard should be rung, or a player may clap his hands under the basket.

Teachers of Classes for the Visually Handicapped

In some schools the visually handicapped are not given the opportunity to participate in the regular classes. In this case the teacher should make the best of what is usually a difficult situation. Ordinarily, a teacher is not trained in physical education, and the school may provide little or no equipment. The heterogeneous age grouping presents a difficult problem in organization. However, sending children out every day for free play denies these youngsters experience in group play which can be obtained only under intelligent adult leadership.

If there is no equipment available, the teacher may have to add a little each year. A gymnasium mat or mattress for tumbling should be placed in the classroom. Perhaps even a short climbing rope or pull-up bar can be erected. A soccer ball (preferably one with bells in it), softball and bat and a utility rubber ball should be obtained as soon as is possible.

By referring to Chapter 13 information can be gained concerning activities recommended for the various grade levels and the amount of time that should be spent on each. Here a limited number of suitable activities will be discussed. First, a teacher should not overlook walking or hiking. Begin slowly, and gradually increase the speed and distance. If possible, make arrangements for swimming at a local pool and bowling at a local bowling establishment. Boys and girls should hang and pull up on horizontal bars and ladders to develop arm strength. Two periods each week should be devoted to rhythms and tumbling. Individual combatives can be an important part of the program. (See Chapter 9.) Children should participate in a number of activities, rather than only a few. Here are a few games which will be found valuable.

Winds

Each of the four sides of a gymnasium or concrete square represent one of the four winds—east, south, west and north. The players stand in the center of the playing area, and the instructor shouts "East," whereupon all the players run to the east wall. The last player to touch the wall is eliminated. The leader then calls another wind and the players run to the designated wall, the last player to reach it being eliminated. Determine a champion for the blind players and another for the partially seeing. Eliminate the champions and run again.

Numbers

Any number of positions can be used, as for example: (a) standing; (b) sitting; (c) lying on stomach; and (d) lying on back. The instructor calls a number, and the last player to take the correct position is eliminated. Continue until a champion is determined. Eliminate the champion and play again. This contest can provide a great deal of fun and exercise if the numbers are called rapidly. This is a good contest for the pupils who need exercise because they are not apt to win in the early rounds.

Spud

The visually handicapped should play spud in an enclosed area such as a gymnasium or tennis court. Place a waste paper basket in one corner of the playing area, enabling sightless players to find the ball quickly. All the players are numbered and stand in a group near the basket, one of them holding a utility rubber ball or basketball. This player calls a number and drops the ball into the basket. All but the one whose number was called immediately scatter. The player called secures the ball as quickly as possible and shouts "Spud!" whereupon all must stand still. The player with the ball tries to hit one of the others with it, while they are clapping their hands. A sightless boy or girl can also locate players by calling them before making a throw. If the thrower misses, one point is scored against him, and all gather around while he calls another number and drops the ball into the basket. When a player is hit, a point is scored against him, and he calls the next number. The player with the lowest score is the winner.

Sport X

An enclosed tennis court or gymnasium provides a suitable area to play sport X. Establish a line 8 or 10 ft. from the end of the area. The runners follow this line in a general way as they run back and forth across the area from fence to fence or wall to wall. Each round trip scores one run. Taking care to equally distribute players with useful vision, two teams are chosen. Sighted players become fielders, while those with little or no vision are runners. The fielders of the opposing teams scatter about the field. A runner of Team A, standing on home base, throws a basketball into the field and starts to run back and forth. In the meantime the fielders of Team A are throwing the ball to one another, keeping it away from fielders of Team B. As soon as a fielder of Team B gains possession of the ball, he throws it across the end line, and the runner of Team A is out. Then a runner of Team B takes his turn and the fielders of his team keep the ball away from the fielders of Team A. A runner can score several runs at one time. The game should be played between ten and fifteen minutes.

Shuffleboard

Some visually handicapped children will be able to play the regular game, but anyone can participate in this modification. Provide a broomstick, tuna fish cans, pie plates, metal rings, etc., for each team. Two contestants, one from each team, step to a line 10 ft. from the wall. Using broomsticks, they push their discs toward the wall. The player whose disc comes closest to the wall without touching it gains one point for his team. A disc which touches the wall cannot score a point.

Snatch the Bacon

All players line up along the same wall or fence. Pair up players according to ability and give them the same number. The instructor stands some distance in front of the line, calls a number, and rings a bell. Two players rush forward toward the sound attempting to touch the bell. The first player to do so gains one point. This is a very good game to develop orientation skills.

Chapter 5

PHYSICAL EDUCATION IN RESIDENTIAL SCHOOLS FOR THE BLIND

THE STATUS OF PHYSICAL EDUCATION IN RESIDENTIAL SCHOOLS FOR THE BLIND

T ODAY RESIDENTIAL SCHOOLS for the blind are placing more emphasis on physical education than ever before. The reason for this is the recognized need of physical fitness that the blind child so obviously has. This has resulted in the organization of programs of physical education in these residential schools which, in most cases, surpass the average public school programs for sighted children. The outstanding feature of this physical education program for blind children is the development of physical fitness. Usually the programs for the boys are better than those offered to the girls.

Most residential schools for the blind offer a program of interscholastic sports for the boys, while the girls participate in play days or track and field competition. In addition, these schools provide physical education for the nonathlete who needs the work most and who stands to benefit the most. This program emphasizes calisthenics, exercises, posture, coordination and balance. Physical rehabilitation of the student with other physical defects besides blindness should also receive consideration. It is the responsibility of the school to provide a program geared to meet the individual needs of each child.

Facilities

One of the most important facilities of a school for the blind is a gymnasium large enough to meet the needs of the student body, which in general averages 150. The gymnasium should be long, rather than square. The main floor should have an area of at least 40 by 80 ft. and be well lighted. In addition there should be at least one room for wrestling and one for gymnastics and weight training, including a punching bag. A minimum of 900 sq. ft. of mats should be provided. If heavy apparatus cannot be placed in a separate room, it should be placed near the wall. Parallel bars, horizontal bars and ladders, side horses, bucks, vaulting boxes, rowing machines, trainer bicycles, trampolines, weight training and body building equipment, punching bags, climbing ropes, basketball goals, peg boards, balance beams and flying rings are desirable pieces of equipment in a physical education program for blind children. Windows should be protected by placing heavy screens on the inside. It is very important to include a swimming pool and two bowling lanes in the gymnasium. Until these facilities are available on the campus, schools should provide for off-campus participation in these sports by students.

A level area for football and softball is essential. Constructing 18-in.—wide asphalt paths on the softball diamond improves the game a great deal for sightless players who can then run the bases by themselves without being called. This independence of action is an important consideration, and the absence of the noise of shouting or calling enables blind fielders to hear a rolling ball better. An asphalt path from the pitcher's mound to home plate should be included, so that a regular softball can be rolled better or a rubber ball bounced to the batter.

A smooth running track with four guide wires should be provided along with jumping pits, metal shot put rings, etc. Guide wires should be stretched 100 yds. without intervening supports and 8- or 10-gauge galvanized, single-stranded wire* is preferred. Usually, these wires are stretched at a height of 3 ft., and some sightless runners touch them lightly with their fingers. Sometimes the runner grasps a trolley which slides easily along a wire. Another idea is that a piece of plastic hose, split so it will fit over the wire, is grasped by the student as he runs. In some cases these wires are stretched overhead, at a height of seven or eight feet. A student grasps a short rope which is tied to a metal ring that slides easily along a wire. Stretching the wires overhead eliminates the interference with playground activities, such as softball.

A large asphalt area should be available for skating, tag games,

---

*For higher tensions, stronger wires may be needed.

etc. Asphalt has the advantage of drying rapidly after a storm. A playground for blind children contains practically the same equipment found on any play area for seeing boys and girls, but to avoid accidents, more care is taken in locating the apparatus. A place to play in rainy weather should be provided. An outdoor pavilion is a very good solution to the problem.

Small Equipment and Gym Suits

Balls should be provided for softball, basketball, football, volleyball, dodgeball, etc. The inflated balls should be painted yellow or bright orange so that partially seeing children can locate them more easily. Large softballs, preferably the 16-in size, should be purchased. These balls are more suitable because they travel shorter distances at reduced speeds and can be more easily seen. Medicine balls and at least one cage ball should be part of the athletic stock. Plenty of jump ropes should be available and also a 50-ft tug-of-war rope. Other items needed are softball bats, shot puts, stop watches, tapes, air pump, megaphone or electric bullhorn.

Students usually furnish their own gym shoes, sweat shirts, swim trunks or suits, skates, stilts, wagons, sleds, toys, etc. However, some state schools provide some of these items. Schools provide members of their competitive teams with uniforms. About half of the residential schools require and provide gym suits for physical education classes on the secondary level. Younger children usually do not change clothes for physical education classes.

The Curriculum

This discussion of curriculm will be based upon surveys made by Williams[1], Wadell[2], and Pollock[3] and the writer's unusually wide experience. Since World War II, there have been some marked changes in the physical education program of many schools for the blind. Most of these changes in curriculum have been made on the secondary rather than the elementary level.

In Grades one, two and three, it is rather common practice for the primary teachers to conduct physical education for their

---

1. F. N. Williams, Huntington College, Huntington, Indiana.
2. Carol Wadell, Perkins School for the Blind, Watertown, Massachusetts.
3. Cathryn Pollock, 100 Memorial Drive, Cambridge, Massachusetts.

pupils. The physical education departments of Michigan, Perkins, Virginia, Ohio, California and some other schools carry on all or part of the activity. In most cases the boys and girls participate together at this level. All of the schools probably offer singing games, rhythmical activities, folk dancing, games of low organization, relays and races, calisthenics and walking. Most of the schools attempt to do some corrective work. Some tumbling and apparatus work is part of most programs, while marching is taught in some schools.

Starting in the intermediate grades, the boys and girls usually take physical education in separate classes. Over three fourths of the schools offer girls ten to fourteen years of age games, relays, calisthenics, corrective exercises, folk and square dancing and swimming. Other activities which are a little less common are tumbling, apparatus work, track and field, softball, hiking and playing on gym scooters. For high school girls less emphasis is placed on games, and more consideration is given to individual sports. Social dancing, bowling, basketball goal shooting, shuffleboard, swimming and the preparation for play days and track and field meets gain importance. About half of the schools spend some time on sports appreciation discussions. Approximately four fifths of the schools have cheerleaders, and the average number is five. Their duties are usually discharged at wrestling meets.

Some activities participated in by girls of all ages are rope jumping, calisthenics, self testing and physical fitness testing activities, roller skating and winter sports in the northern states and Canada.

Activities deemed most beneficial for blind girls are rope jumping, roller skating, bowling, swimming, hiking, dancing, and track and field events. Physical fitness testing and the development of pride in one's fitness, as well as her figure, is very desirable. Play days and interscholastic track meets, which are now held once or twice a year, should be scheduled much oftener. It would be most advantageous to schedule these events with local public schools. The blind girls gain much from this type of association, and it does much for public education. One or two opportunities a year to gain these distinct advantages are not nearly enough.

For boys over ten years of age, four fifths or more of the schools offer calisthenics, games, wrestling, track and field, gymnastics, tumbling, softball, social dancing and swimming. Activities conducted by one half to two thirds of the schools are basketball, bowling, volleyball and square dancing. Other activities which are

FIGURE 4. Gymnastics at the New Mexico School for the Visually Handicapped.

FIGURE 4

somewhat less common are hiking, marching, horseshoes, soccer and football. A few schools offer cross-country running, archery and weight training. About four fifths of the schools for the blind develop teams in interscholastic wrestling, and nearly as many compete in track and field meets. Approximately one third of the schools field bowling teams and swimming teams. Gymnastic teams and partially seeing basketball teams represent about ten schools. Perhaps it should be pointed out that most of the activities carried on in schools for the blind do not require balls or quick movement of the eyes to follow flying objects. Some activities, such as basketball and softball, are participated in by the partially seeing, or major adaptations are made for sightless players.

It will be noted that many more opportunities are given to the boys than to the girls for association with students from other schools. The program should be extended to boys and girls in residential schools who are ready for this type of experience but do not now get it. This can be done in play days held with public schools and through scouting and church associations. Children who are ready for the experience should be encouraged to attend camps other than those for blind children.

Excluding interscholastic athletics, the time allotted to physical education on the secondary level in schools for the blind ranges from one to five hours per week. The median is three and a half hours. The length of the class period is usually forty-five to sixty minutes. Two thirds of the schools hold physical education classes for older boys and girls during school hours, while the rest schedule classes later in the afternoon. In addition, interscholastic teams usually practice after school hours. Some schools do not schedule physical education daily. The President's Council of Physical Fitness has consistently urged all schools to require daily participation in physical education by a student. This policy has been recently reaffirmed by the legislature of the State of California.

Two areas in which schools for the blind need to place more emphasis are: (a) conducting more activities in which blind children come into direct contact with boys and girls who have normal vision; and (b) developing skills which can be used when participating in activities with sighted people. It is desirable that success should be possible without making concessions to blind individuals or drastically modifying the activity. If activities make a blind child feel peculiar and different from his seeing peers, they are less desirable.

Factors Influencing the Physical Education Program

The most important factor in the physical education program is the leader. The success or failure of the physical education program depends upon the quality of its leadership. The best results in physical education can be obtained only if students are willing to extend themselves completely in strenuous physical activities and to make every effort to perform exercises in prescribed form. Only the best leadership can inspire boys and girls to cooperate to this extent.

The most essential quality of the physical education teacher is the possession of abounding energy and enthusiasm. The leader should exemplify the things he seeks to teach. Special requirements of a teacher for the blind are patience, resourcefulness, likeable personality and a pleasing voice.

A successful teacher commands the respect of his students. He wins their respect by his sincerity, integrity, determination, sense of justice, energy and force of character. The teacher must also know his subject matter, including special methods for the blind. He should have a good understanding of psychology and the anatomy, physiology and hygiene of the eye. The limitations of the blind require an expert teacher.

Should a visually handicapped teacher be employed for physical education? Only 20/200 vision is necessary to conduct classes. Generally speaking, a partially seeing teacher with the necessary training and personal qualifications seems to be the best person for the work. Due to his handicap, he is more apt to understand the problems involved. However, some of the best teachers in the field today are not visually handicapped.

Since World War II, physical education teachers in schools for the blind have become much more stable. Three fifths of the schools have a physical educator who has been on the job for ten or more years, a number of these being partially sighted. These veteran teachers of blind children are usually found in boys' physical education, but there are a few in girls' departments. This increased stability has played a very important role in the overall development of physical education for children in residential schools for the blind.

Other factors which influence the physical education program are: (a) the amount of financial backing; (b) available facilities; (c) the enthusiasm and backing of the principal and the general teaching staff; and (d) the climate.

The presence or absence of classes for corrective work can make a big difference in a physical education teacher's approach in his regular classes. When those who need corrective work are scheduled together in smaller classes, they benefit more, as do the regular students. One or two students who do not fit into an activity gain little benefit from it and tend to disrupt the rest of the class by slowing down the tempo.

Motivation

Since blind children tend to be sedentary, more motivation is required in their physical training than in programs for seeing boys and girls. One of the best ways to enliven and motivate the physical education program is through interscholastic competition. In wrestling, for example, the younger boys begin to practice for the day when they can be on the team, and the older boys work hard to be worthy representatives of the school. Teams should be formed within physical education classes for daily activities, once a week or at least every month. Although team competition is one of the oldest motivations, it is still one of the best. Children will work hard to put on public demonstrations of gymnastics and other activities.

Girls' teachers find that a point system, based upon participation in activities, skills, sportsmanship, etc., is satisfactory. (See Appendix H for the point system used at the Perkins School for the Blind.) The girls work to win letters at the end of the year. Most girls know by now that a certain amount of skill in sports helps to make them more popular. It can be pointed out that exercise improves the general health of the body, resulting in better complexion and physical appearance.

Awarding badges or certificates for passing certain tests in swimming, track and field or tumbling appeals to many students. Each spring some of the schools conduct decathlons, using the achievement scales in Chapter 12. Since one event is practiced and tested for each week, the decathlon lasts ten weeks. Students of all ages have an opportunity to win the top awards, so interest is high at all age levels. Boys and girls can also measure their abilities against the norms for each event. Most children will want to practice to bring their performance up to the average. Children will pride themselves upon making improvement from one month to another or from one year to another.

Class Organization

Blind children are usually grouped for physical education according to school grades. This procedure will be successful only when all weaker students with poor coordination are placed in corrective classes. Unfortunately, this practice is not followed in a number of schools for the blind where weak children retard the progress of the rest of the class.

The size of the class should depend upon the kind of instruction to be given. Where a great deal of individual work is to be done in teaching apparatus work, tumbling, dance steps and corrective exercises, the class should be limited to eight children. Twice this number is satisfactory for games and contests. A few schools for the blind have classes of thirty to forty students. Obviously, classes of this size are too large for the blind individual to make much progress.

Children should have at least half an hour of vigorous physical activity every day. Beyond this, there is no agreement as to what should be done in the physical education period. After twenty-five years of experience, the writer has developed some guide lines. First, allow ten minutes for changing clothes at the beginning of the period and another ten minutes for dressing at the end of the period. Second, devote the first ten minutes of the activity period to calisthenics and conditioning exercises such as rope climbing, distance running, etc. Third, use only activities which are vigorous and interesting. Fourth, conduct activities in which the totally blind can really take part. Fifth, conduct vigorous activities such as games, tumbling, dancing, swimming and relays, for at least twenty minutes. Sixth, physical education should receive as much time in the curriculum as any other subject. This means thirty minutes daily for primary boys and girls, and forty-five to sixty minutes every day for children over ten years of age.

Physical educators in residential schools[4] seem to favor a daily change of activity. Since children remain in these schools many years, it is possible to develop a progression of skills which will result in a well-rounded program for each boy and girl. In this type of scheduling best use of facilities can be made in relation to changing weather conditions. Also children are apt to come to class in a better frame of mind.

Each school should establish a definite policy concerning excusing students from physical education activities. First, some written explanation from the nurse or superintendent should be sent to the physical education instructor. Second, if a student is in school, he should report to the physical education class. When he has a written excuse from activity, he should sit on a bench and study his academic lessons. If a student is recovering from an illness or an injury, he should be assigned modified activity which will benefit rather than harm him.

---

4. *Proceedings, American Association of Instructors of the Blind,* 1958. P. 84.

In grading, most physical educators of the blind set up requirements in various sports. All grades should be given on an individual basis. If a pupil with little ability tries hard, he is given an average grade. Most instructors consider attitude to be very important and value it as one third of the grade

Corrective Physical Education

During the early years of life, children of normal vision are naturally very active. Parents often refuse to allow blind children to participate in normal physical activity because of fear that they may be injured. This inactivity prevents normal physical development and results in low vitality and physical stamina. Many children enter schools for the blind lacking in confidence and neuro-muscular control. Their posture is often poor, and emotional and muscular energy may find an outlet in "blindisms"[5]—finger tapping, head shaking, body rocking, eye poking, etc. As pointed out over a hundred years ago by Dr. Howe,[6] a little common sense and emotional control will go a long way toward preventing and correcting these conditions. If the child enters school at an early age, a great deal can be accomplished in the correction of physical weaknesses and defects. Unfortunately, many blind children are over ten years of age before they receive proper training. Even the simple activity of much walking in early childhood can be an effective prevention.

Again it should be emphasized that parental overprotection of blind children usually results in marked retardation in their physical development. Since one third of blind girls[7] and one fourth of sightless boys have been seriously hampered in their development by overprotective parents, it is very important to point out the harm done. The more parents shield children and prevent them from moving around, the more they retard the normal development of their offspring. Most of the children in the corrective classes in the residential schools come from homes that have overprotected them.

---

5. LOWENFELD, BERTHOLD: *Our Blind Children*. Springfield, Ill., Charles C Thomas, 1964, pp. 103-104.

6. *Perkins Report*, 1841. P. 7.

7. BUELL, CHARLES: *Motor Performance of Visually Handicapped Children*. Ann Arbor, Michigan, 1950, p. 55.

Faulty preschool training, though it is most important, is not the only reason for the low physical vigor of many blind children. Other principal reasons for this are: (a) the fact that lack of vision tends to curtail physical activity; and (b) additional defects or weaknesses resulting from an illness, accident or congenital condition causing blindness. Special schools provide thorough medical examinations and competent health supervision of their pupils. It is desirable that the physical education teacher be present at the health examination of his pupils. At this time the physician can point out limitations that should be observed and prescribe exercises for corrective cases. The physical education teacher should not attempt corrective work without direction from the school physician.

In every school there are a number of children who are in need of corrective exercises. Others should have modified activities. For example, those with weak hearts and the more serious cases of myopia and glaucoma should not participate in strenuous exercise. Most doctors agree that "restricted" children should have some activity. If the school has a program of modified activities, only a very few children need be assigned to complete rest. A doctor must be cognizant of the type of work done in the modified class so that he can make his recommendations intelligently. It is the responsibility of teachers to put the recommended program into effect. If the corrective program of the physical education department is to be successful, the entire school staff must stress posture and see that "restricted" children do not overdo during the hours after school.

A special class should be formed for corrective work. Since the students eligible for such a class are in various grades, scheduling difficulties usually arise. However, every effort should be made to give "restricted" children an activity period. It has been said that, in the education of the blind, health should come first and all else will follow. Lack of sight is a serious handicap and should not be increased by the additional disabilities of poor health and low neuro-muscular development if this can be avoided.

Corrective work in many schools is limited to exercises of the more formal type. Calisthenics have their place and can do much to improve posture and build up stamina and strength. However, to be complete, a program of corrective physical education must also include recreational activities such as swimming, games, tumbling, relays, rhythms and dancing. If healthy people need these activities, so do physically handicapped individuals.

The must common problem faced in corrective physical education is the development of better body mechanics or posture. Actually, only a small part of this development can be expected to take place during the physical education class period. A student must exercise weak muscles from time to time during the day. Encouragement by all teachers and parents is usually needed to attain best results. However, the physical educator can make the student understand what is needed and can help motivate him to accomplish it. Giving encouragement rather than nagging or scolding is the best approach. Teachers should remind students to "sit tall" and "stand tall," rather than command, "shoulders back." The latter position is unnatural to hold and results in a hollow back.

To assume good posture, one must first know what it is. In good posture the head is held high with chin slightly tucked in, shoulders made as wide as possible rather than thrown back, the chest held up rather than thrown out, the lower back flattened, and the knees straight but not stiff. In sitting, the hips should be far enough back on the seat to allow the thighs to support the weight of the body. A blind child can test his posture by backing up against a wall, so that his heels, hips, shoulders and head touch the wall. The curve in the small of the back should be so slight that a flat hand cannot be passed between the back and the wall.

Unfortunately, authorities do not agree on how good posture is best attained. Helpful suggestions will be found in books by Fait[8] and Howland[9]. Some helpful exercises are listed in Appendix I.

SUMMARY

Sir Francis Campbell once said: "The education of the blind whether literary, musical, or technical will not be crowned with

8. FAIT, HOLLIS: *Adapted Physical Education.* Philadelphia, W. B. Saunders, 1960, pp. 88-117.
9. HOWLAND, IVALCLARE: *Body Alignment in Fundamental Motor Skills.* New York, Exposition Press, 1953.

practical success unless based upon a thorough system of physical education." For the most part, residential schools for the blind have met the challenge. Adequate physical fitness is being developed in most cases along with other desirable characteristics gained from physical training. However, there is another goal that must be achieved. Skills must be developed in visually handicapped individuals so that they will feel at ease with people who have normal vision. Competitive athletics and play days are a step in the right direction, but these opportunities must be extended to many more pupils in the student body than now is the case. The physical education department can make a tremendous contribution toward the socialization of blind children. When this is done, the greatest weakness in residential schools for the blind will be overcome.

Chapter 6

RECREATIONAL AND LEISURE-TIME ACTIVITIES—A GUIDE FOR PARENTS

ACTUALLY most leisure-time activities commonly engaged in by children are feasible for blind boys and girls. Sometimes slight modifications must be made so that blind children can successfully participate. In almost all cases it is desirable for blind boys and girls to integrate in the activities of other children at school, in organizations, clubs, in the neighborhood and family. Only such modifications should be made for blind participants which do not interfere with the enjoyment of the activity by boys and girls with normal vision. It is important to remember that one derives much more benefit from activities as a participant than as a spectator. Do not let a blind child be a "watcher" only.

A number of activities will be mentioned below with suggestions as to how visually handicapped children can fit into them. However, a word of caution is necessary. Not all blind children will be capable of gaining value from all these activities, any more than would all boys and girls. In other words, the activities in which an individual should participate will depend upon his capabilities and interests. Recreation should be fitted to the individual and not the individual fitted to a recreational program. To be successful, we must recognize individual differences.

As a parent selects activities with his child and the way he will participate in them, one point should be kept uppermost in mind. Visually handicapped boys and girls should be treated primarily as children, not as blind individuals. Continued inactivity is harmful for anyone. A blind child should receive only the protection which reasonable parents offer to other children.

It is well to remember that bumps and scratches affect only the skin and immediate tissues and do not injure the system like "the rust of inaction."

The welfare and success of blind children can be affected by whether or not they participate in activities at the same age as do children who have normal vision. In other words, a parent should not delay or postpone activities for his child because of blindness. Teachers of blind children can testify very vigorously to the harm that results from delay, because they have seen many unfortunate cases of it.

Certainly one of the first activities engaged in by all children is walking, and this should include blind youngsters as well. They should be encouraged to walk short distances by themselves, gradually increasing in length. On longer trips a parent may walk hand in hand with his blind child as he would with his other younger children. There are a number of advantages to be gained from walking by anyone, particularly blind children. (See page 92.)

CLASSIFICATION OF ACTIVITIES

Recreational and leisure-time activities of children may be divided into six classifications. There are community, organizational, commercial entertainment, neighborhood, family and individual activities. This is a very loose classification and is used only to cover a wide field of information. A child may participate in an activity such as swimming as a member of his family, with a neighborhood group or in an organization such as the YMCA.

Community Activities

There are many activities available in a community which may be attended free of charge or for a small fee. Practically all of these activities will be enjoyed by blind children. In many cases educational benefits will result.

For example, let's go to a parade. Blind children will listen intently to the bands and thus feel the excitement of the occasion. If there are floats, marching units or equestrian groups, these can be described in a manner that will be meaningful to a sightless child. Perhaps at the beginning or end of the parade a child can actually examine some of the floats. Also, being a part of the group gives the blind child a feeling of belonging. Later on he can discuss with his friends what they experienced, and this contributes to his social integration.

Most everyone attends a state or county fair. Blind children will examine what they can by touch, by hearing, by smell and taste and again will gain much from good descriptions. Fourth of July celebrations and other such occasions can mean much to a visually handicapped boy or girl. Just hearing the firecrackers explode will be great excitement.

Don't overlook the opportunities offered by the public park. There may be a museum, aquarium or zoo. Senses other than sight will bring the blind child many impressions. A perceptive companion can add valuable information. Such a companion need not always be an adult person. Often another youngster can explain things better to his blind companion because they live in the same world for which adults do not always have a good understanding. Sometimes keys can be purchased to turn on descriptive records. Also those in charge of such facilities are often willing to let blind children feel objects in cases or animals in pens. Some community parks are erecting fairylands or storylands which are a delight to all children. Such parks usually have a swimming pool. Swimming has many values for a blind boy or girl, and it is not more dangerous for them than for anyone else. Older blind children, under guidance, will gain a thrill and plenty of exercise from rowing a boat on the park lake. Younger children will certainly enjoy riding in such a boat.

Organizational Activities

Among organizational activities, some of the best are found in scouting—Cub Scouts, Boy Scouts, Girl Scouts, Brownies, Camp fire Girls, etc. It is desirable that not more than one or two visually handicapped children join a single unit. There are Braille handbooks available, and some modifications are usually made in the requirements for qualifying for badges. Blind children obtain just as much from scouting as anyone if they are permitted to participate fully in activities.

Church organizations, such as the Protestant Youth Group, Catholic Youth Organization and others, have as much to offer to blind children as to those who have sight. In fact, experience has shown that these organizations are more willing to accept blind individuals than are many others. Many blind girls and boys in the United States belong either to the YWCA or the YMCA and

FIGURE 5. Girls swimming and diving at the Texas School for the Blind.

receive much value from such memberships. In addition to physical activities and crafts, dramatics, ballroom dancing and folk dancing may be enjoyed in this setting as well as elsewhere.

There are interest clubs that offer many opportunities, particularly for children in their teens. Youth hostel groups sometimes provide programs for visually handicapped children. By using tandem bicycles, a number of blind boys and girls participate in some activities of a youth hostel group in San Diego, California. Amateur groups interested in radio, science, foreign language, future homemakers, commercial, chess and many other subjects have been widely organized. For the partially sighted boy or girl, photography and subjects that require little useful vision are possible.

Throughout the United States agencies and organizations for the blind often offer opportunities for children's recreation. Many of these are segregated programs, but some organizations offer activities in which visually handicapped boys and girls mingle with sighted children in order to provide opportunity for social integration. A parent who is considering a program including blind children only should carefully evaluate his son or daughter to determine whether or not it is best for the child. If a blind child can get along reasonably well in school and neighborhood with sighted peers, a segregated program is probably not desirable for him. In other words, some children will benefit from an agency program, while others will not.

Some activities offered by agencies for the visually handicapped are camp, day camp, nursery school, teen-age activities such as sports, parties, trips, etc. A number of these programs are well planned and carried out under able leadership.

Commercial Entertainment

Commercial entertainment offers many opportunities for recreation to blind children. Roller skating, ice skating, bowling and horseback riding are popular among blind boys and girls. Totally blind bowlers can purchase a portable guide rail to assist them.[1]

---

1. Guide rails for bowling may be purchased from the American Foundation for the Blind, 15 West 16th Street, New York, New York.

Most of the concessions at a playland can be fully enjoyed by blind children depending, of course, on their age and readiness for the specific activity.

Attending sporting events brings much pleasure to blind boys and girls. If the contest is being broadcast, they take along their transistor radios. Otherwise, a running description will be most helpful. The reaction of the crowd, the hot dogs and the thrill of being present at an exciting athletic contest mean much to anyone. Blind children have their favorite teams and heroes, and interest in sports is very high with them. In fact, being able to discuss sports knowledgeably with others is often an opener for continued relationships.

Attending motion pictures is a common practice among blind boys and girls. People with normal vision often find it difficult to believe how much can be gained from hearing sounds and dialogues in pictures. They forget that listening to the radio places anyone essentially in the same position. However, sometimes scenes in moving pictures may require a brief description. There are some films which are not particularly suited for totally blind people, such as cartoons and slapstick comedies. However, partially sighted children will enjoy these features.

Concerts are being mentioned only because they obviously present no problem. Attending the theater can be made much more meaningful if some information about the stage setting, costumes, time of the play, etc. can be given beforehand.

Neighborhood Activities

It is certainly most desirable that a blind child participate in neighborhood activities. This is sometimes difficult to achieve. The mother of a blind child can help by inviting neighborhood children into her home for various activities. She may offer this initially with the idea of taking care of these children so that their mothers can go shopping or have a free afternoon. As time goes on the blind child will be invited to homes of other children. At these gatherings any child will be more acceptable if he plays an instrument or has athletic ability and a pleasant personality with interesting conversation.

For some ideas on party games that are suitable for blind as well as sighted children, Buell's *Recreation for the Blind*[2] will be found helpful. One may take any game book and find suitable games and activities, some of which need no or only slight adaptations.

Then there are the active games of the neighborhood. Most every child plays softball in season. Rolling the ball on the ground to a blind batter does not destroy any interest in the game for the other players. A teammate can run the bases with a sightless boy. If a blind fielder catches a rolling ball, it should be counted as an out, similar to a fly ball.

Kick baseball is popular in many areas. If a blind child has an audible ball,[3] he can much more easily adapt himself to the game. The audible ball can be used for other activities, such as shooting baskets. (See Chapter 7 for other sports.)

In hide and go seek a blind player can pair up with one who has sight. This does not in any way interfere with the enjoyment of the game by other players.

In addition to pairing up players, there are other hints as to how blind boys and girls can fit into the games and sports of the neighborhood. Where direct contact exists, such as in wrestling, there is no problem. A limited playing area, such as a small lawn, is very helpful. Blind children should be encouraged to participate in activities where sounds exist.

A wise parent will be able to find many ways in which a blind child can fit into neighborhood activities so that it will not interfere with the interests of others. All that is needed is a good understanding of the effects of blindness and confidence in the abilities of the child. One important point to remember is that usually a parent and his blind child must take the initiative and not expect the neighbors to come to them. Consultation with those experienced in work for the blind will be helpful.

Family Activities

A blind child should be included in family activities just as

---

2. BUELL, CHARLES: *Recreation for the Blind.* New York, American Foundation for the Blind, 1951, 40 pp.

3. A soccer ball with a bell in it can be purchased from American Foundation for the Blind, 15 West 16th Street, New York, New York 10011. Price $5.90 including postage.

much as any of the other children. Some mothers, for example, leave their blind children in the automobile while they shop. Just think what a blind child could learn by touch in a grocery store, a hardware store or a variety store.

Table games are possible for the blind, but they are modified somewhat. Braille playing cards are used, and dominoes are made with raised spots. Checkers and chess are played on boards with raised squares, and the checkers are round or square, while the chess figures are marked by a pin on the top to differentiate black and white men. These and other table games can be purchased from the American Foundation for the Blind, 15 West 16th Street, New York 11, New York.

Every family should do some camping together, and a blind child will enjoy this greatly. Blind children look forward to trips to the snow and to winter sports. Fishing is just as popular for the blind as for anyone else. The companionship, the exhilarating feeling of being in the open and other features of hiking appeal to boys and girls.

Tandem bicycles bring all the benefits of the sport of cycling to blind children. A blind youngster enjoys cycling near or far with another member of the family.

Some families erect basketball goals in the backyard or on the garage. If bells are attached to the goal, a blind child can enjoy shooting goals. A few of these have been even fitted with electric buzzers.

A pull-up bar placed in the backyard can be enjoyed by all children, including those who have no sight. Likewise, a short climbing rope or swinging rope offers valuable arm exercise as well as enjoyment.

Don't discard sightseeing and tours as a recreational activity. Fortunately, vision is not a requirement for one to experience the thrill of standing upon the spot where history was made. If there is not a guide with a regular commentary, descriptive details can be given by a seeing person.

All children yearn to do some simple cooking. A wise mother will include her blind child in such activities. A blind boy or girl often knows foods only in prepared or cooked form. He should also learn about them "in the raw" and will enjoy cooking, including the tasting. Some older children may find it desirable to use cooking aids which may be purchased from the American Foundation for the Blind. Also, recipes are available in Braille and on phonograph records.

Individual Activities

There are many activities that appeal to various blind boys and girls. First of all, one will think of listening to radio and television. It is comparatively easy to obtain the loan of a talking book which will bring many educational benefits and enjoyment. Reading Braille books and magazines has much to offer. However, any child should not devote an excessive amount of his time to such activities because it will limit the time for being active.

Naturally, playing with toys is just as important for blind children as for those who can see. A good understanding of the effects of blindness will enable a parent to select suitable toys for his visually handicapped son or daughter. There are a number of puzzles that do not require vision to solve.

Blind boys and girls should be encouraged to care for a pet. Very young children will enjoy the feeling of having a companion. As a child grows older he should gradually assume more and more responsibility for the care of his pet. In the beginning he will probably feed the cat or dog and find a comfortable place for it to rest. Naturally he must be kind to an animal if he expects it to be his companion. Later he should be expected to keep the animal and its living quarters clean. A child should teach the animal obedience so that he and his pet will be acceptable to his family and friends. Caring daily for an animal can develop in the child a sense of responsibility at an age earlier than might be expected.

Many blind children will enjoy planting and caring for a simple garden of vegetables or fragrant flowers. Many blind people find guide wires helpful in planting and caring for a garden, particularly when rows are desired. As a child grows older he can assume greater responsibilities and attempt more difficult tasks.

Hobbies have much to offer anyone, including blind children, who sometimes have more than the normal amount of leisure-time on their hands. However, one must be careful not to devote an excessive amount of time to hobbies, because participation in a wide variety of activities is desirable. Some of the activities more commonly engaged in by blind individuals are leathercraft, weaving, basketry, ceramics, woodwork, needlecraft, crocheting and knitting. These and other activities are described in some detail in Ritter's *Hobbies of Blind Adults*,[4] which mentions many helpful hints that apply to children as well.

A young child or one less skilled will start with simple handicraft projects and gradually advance to more difficult work. For example, there are simple looms for weaving and projects in leather that require little skill. In woodworking, a child might first drive a nail into balsa wood. When he becomes adept at this, harder woods may be used. Older blind boys can safely use power tools. Obviously, they must have a thorough knowledge of the machine and a healthy respect for the damage it can do.

For sewing, blind girls will probably want to use self-threading needles or needle-threaders, which can be purchased in large department stores. Older blind girls can safely operate sewing machines, for which special attachments and guards are sometimes purchased.

Marked tapes and other hobby aids are available from the American Foundation for the Blind. These will often enable a blind boy or girl to more fully enjoy some hobbies and eliminate some of the dangers in others.

SUMMARY

Well-planned recreation programs for children will develop in them a desire to play and freedom of action which will be carried into adulthood. Such programs should strive to teach visually handicapped boys and girls to express themselves naturally so that they will be better equipped to take a normal place in society. It is important that children learn activities for use in leisure time. Recreation programs make possible a fuller life for children and adults.

---

4. RITTER, CHARLES: *Hobbies of Blind Adults.* New York, American Foundation for the Blind, 1953, 52 pp.

Chapter 7

SPORTS AND INTERSCHOLASTIC COMPETITION FOR THE BLIND

THE VALUE OF COMPETITION with teams from other schools is now generally accepted. It is one of the best ways to motivate the development of muscular strength, speed, endurance, fighting spirit, mental balance and teamwork. In public schools only a small percentage of the pupils benefit from such a program, but in special schools, with their small enrollments, practically every high school boy is on the team. Through these activities a respect for the blind athlete is built up in the minds of sighted opponents. Competition enables blind boys and girls to make acquaintances and friendships with those who have normal vision. It gives students in special schools more confidence in themselves and a great deal of satisfaction to be able to participate in the activities of other school children. The athletic awards which the blind athletes receive are only a minor part of interscholastic competition.

About four fifths of the schools for the blind enter into some type of athletic competition. There are four athletic associations of schools for the blind. Besides being an important source of motivation in athletics, these organizations stimulate social development as well. Several social events are usually held before and after the athletic competition.

Not all schools for the blind which sponsor teams belong to these athletic associations. Most of the members of the associations carry on the bulk of their competition outside of these organizations. In other words, most of the interscholastic competition in special schools is carried on with local public junior and senior high schools. One reason for this is that special schools are usually located hundreds of miles apart. Another consideration is that more values in socialization can come from this type of competition. More teams are developed in wrestling than in any other sport, but track and field teams are only slightly less numerous. Approximately one third of the schools for the blind field bowling teams and swimming teams. Gymnastic teams and teams of partially seeing basketball players represent about ten special schools.

In public schools, competition is most common in softball or baseball, football, basketball and track and field. Let us consider these and other sports for the blind.

Softball

In softball, as it is now played in most schools for the blind, the ball is rolled to a sightless batter. The batter listens to the ball rolling on the ground and hits it. He then runs to a teammate who is calling him on first base. In schools for the blind which have asphalt paths, the runner moves from base to base by himself without being called. When a blind fielder catches a rolling ball, it is considered as a put out.

Some of the eastern schools for the blind use a large inflated rubber ball which is bounced to the batter who hits it with his hand. In some places, the sightless batter sets a ball on a tee before hitting it. Blind boys get a big thrill when they can hit a ball thrown to them in the air. The pitcher must tell the batter when to swing his bat. In five turns at bat a sightless batter usually hits fairly two or three times. By holding the ball in the hand, some blind boys can hit fly balls or grounders to be fielded by other players.

A modified form of kick baseball is popular in some areas. In California a soccer ball with bells in it is used. If a blind fielder catches a rolling ball, it is counted as an out. Since older boys become quite adept at this, the game has become a favorite. A blind batter places the ball on home plate, kicks it and then runs to first base.

Another modification of softball is a game called gutterball. The pitcher rolls the ball to the batter in a trough such as a street gutter. Baseball rules are followed with these exceptions.

1. There are no base runners.
2. A grounder cleanly trapped by a sightless player is a fly ball, and the batter is out.
3. The value of a hit is determined by the time that elapses

before a fielder returns the ball to the pitcher's mound. This
is determined by the umpire's standard count.

Under 6—out   15 to 17—triple
6 to 11—single   18 and over—home run
12 to 14—double

With slight modifications hit pin baseball is played by blind
children. It has the advantage of being an active game that can
be played in small gymnasiums during the winter months. Base
lines should be made long enough (at least 20 ft) so that scoring
will not be too easy. Large Indian clubs are set up on first, second
and third bases. A soccer ball, preferably with bells in it, is rolled
on the ground to partially seeing batters, while the sightless batter
kicks the ball after it has been placed on home plate. After kicking
the ball, the batter runs the circuit of bases (passing on the outside of all pins) attempting to reach the home base before he is
put out. A boy with some vision runs with a blind batter. The
partially seeing boys field the ball and try to knock the Indian
clubs down before the runner crosses home plate. If a fly ball is
caught, the runner is out. If a sightless fielder catches a rolling
ball, it is an out. Small gymnasiums have the advantage that the
ball cannot go very far before rebounding from a wall.

For many years the author has played the World Series in his
gym classes. Teams are chosen, and each boy represents one of the
regulars on the two competing big league clubs. The fielding positions and the batting orders selected by the major league managers
are followed. This has helped many blind boys to better understand and thus become interested in the annual classic of the great
American game.

Football

The most common form of football played in schools for the
blind is a kicking game. One team kicks off from the middle of
the field, and the ball is kicked back and forth until one team
scores. A point is scored when the ball is kicked in the air over
the goal line and is not caught by a defensive player. The members
of each team kick in order. A kick is made from the point where
the defensive team stops the bounding or rolling ball. If a partially

seeing boy catches the ball on the fly, he takes three steps forward before the ball is kicked.

In the regular game of football the runner shouts "Hike" as the ball is snapped or placed in his hands by the center. The runner continues to shout, and the defensive players run toward the sound to make the tackle. The game is best played on a field that is about 10 yds wide and 40 or 50 yds long. In this type of play, serious injuries are almost unknown.

Today, none of the schools for the blind field football teams. In combined schools, the partially seeing boys sometimes play on the deaf boys' teams. However, for thirty-five years the Michigan School for the Blind developed interscholastic football teams. (See p. 27.)

Basketball

Before 1950 the partially seeing boys and girls of the Michigan School for the Blind played interscholastic basketball for about thirty-five years, but in recent years the sport has been participated in only on an intramural basis. Other schools for the blind have entered competition from time to time when a person on the staff wished to volunteer his time and efforts to develop a team. Since partially seeing players are at a distinct disadvantage in this fast game, a great deal of practice is required to compete on a basis that is anywhere near equal to the performance of a team whose members have normal vision. Visually handicapped players should concentrate on developing dribbling and short passing sequences to score. A zone defense will be found more practical and effective for teams of partially seeing players. With proper training, a school for the blind team will usually win about one fourth to one third of its games. In some cases, the visually handicapped players may be a little older than their opponents.

Shooting baskets has long been a favorite pastime of partially seeing and sightless boys. Sometimes intramural competition is held in free throwing. An audible basketball goal locator is now available[1] which can do much to improve the shooting accuracy

---

1. American Printing House for the Blind, 1839 Frankfort Avenue, Louisville, Kentucky. Price of locator is $18.50.

of a sightless player. A less expensive device is a bell hung on or near the basket with a cord extending to the floor.

Track and Field

Track meets for the blind usually include two dashes, standing broad jump, standing hop, step and jump, standing triple jump, standing high jump, one-step high jump, rope climb, shot put, football throw for distance, tug-of-war and tandem running. In the latter event, a sightless runner pairs up with one who has some or all of his vision. The distances commonly used for competition are the mile and two-mile runs, but some runners have participated in cross-country meets. In schools for the blind, guide wires, stretched 100 yds. without intervening supports, make running possible and practical for sightless boys and girls. If there are no other loud noises a whistle can be blown in front of a blind runner. This will serve as a satisfactory guide in dashes. For endurance running, a sightless athlete may follow a bicycle or motor scooter driven by a sighted companion. A few schools for the blind have indoor tracks with rails upon which the fingers can be lightly touched to gain direction.

There has been a revival of the marathon idea. Athletic clubs and schools total the number of miles run by members or students during the month. These totals are compared (sometimes by mail) with other clubs and schools. It is a motivation device that might well be used in schools and classes for the blind.

By 1960 it became evident that athletes with visual impairments were competing under different rules in various sections of the United States. At this time a national committee was set up to standardize the rules. Within recent years these rules have been adopted throughout the United States. This has made it possible to establish national records in track and field for visually handicapped boys. The records listed here are those which have been accepted by the Track and Field Committee of the American Association of Instructors of the Blind. Application forms for such records may be obtained from Dr. Charles Buell, California School for the Blind, Berkeley, California.

NATIONAL TRACK AND FIELD RECORDS
FOR VISUALLY HANDICAPPED ATHLETES

Event	Record	Name	School	Year
50 yd dash	5.4	Hambrick	Arkansas	1957
		Sykes	Missouri	1958
75 yd dash	7.7	Little	Arkansas	1962
Standing broad jump	10-6½	Caballero	Louisiana	1964
Triple jump	32-4½	Ogburn	Arkansas	1956
Hop, step and jump	30-10	Johnson	Maryland	1962
Standing high jump	5-3 1/4	Benson	Mississippi	1965
		Machac	Texas	1964
One-step high jump	5-3 3/4	Casabianca	New York Institute	1964
Running high jump	5 8	Benson	Mississippi	1965
Basketball throw	127-8	McKenzie	New Mexico	1957
12 lb shot put	49-9½	J. Watson	Texas	1963
8 lb shot put	51-2½	Brooks	Overbrook	1964
Football throw	156-3	Booth	Texas	1960
Run. football throw	194-7	Forader	Connecticut	1960
Half mile run	2:14.7	McCauley	Perkins	1961
1-mile tandem	5:41.0	Case	Mississippi	1965
		Kenderson	Mississippi	1965
2-mile tandem	11:31.1	McCauley	Perkins	1962
		Hagneier	Perkins	1962

Play Days

Most schools for the blind hold play days of some type for girls and sometimes for boys. Play days are held in schools for the blind, with other schools for the blind and with public school children. Games, relays and races are usually part of the program along with sightseeing and social events.

Perhaps a brief description of a play day held by the New Mexico School for the Visually Handicapped on Washington's Birthday will convey some idea of this type of activity. The guests were twenty-four girls from Tularosa High School. The event opened at 8:30 in the morning, when hostesses were assigned to each guest, teams lined up and team emblems selected. After refreshments a practice period was held from 10:00 to 11:45. At noon a buffet luncheon was served. The decorations, preparation and serving were projects of the home economics classes. After lunch the guests were conducted on a tour of the grounds. The play day events started at 2:00 in the afternoon. Events included single stunts, pyramids, dances, couple and combat stunts, all given patriotic names. Each school also presented a special skit or dance.

Wrestling

Within the past twenty years there has been a tremendous growth in interscholastic wrestling in the public schools of the United States. In schools for the blind a similar growth of the sport has taken place. Today there are about 500 visually handicapped wrestlers, most of them in schools for the blind, participating in interscholastic and intercollegiate competition. Wrestling is a major sport for blind boys, while it remains as a minor sport in many public high schools. Due to the difference in emphasis, a number of the special schools are able to defeat teams of even the largest public high schools. Man for man, special schools usually compete on an equal basis with other schools. However, many schools for the visually handicapped cannot fill all of the ten to twelve weight classes, and according to the rules, must forfeit points to the opposing team. The average high school enrollment, fourteen years and older, is about twenty-five boys, so it is obvious that only the larger schools are able to fill all of the required weight divisions. In spite of this, teams of blind wrestlers win many more meets than they lose. Teams from residential schools have won state championships (see page 39), and every year some of these teams are among the leaders in the state meets.

Blind wrestlers have won individual championships at all levels of competition—junior and senior high school, university and AAU. A blind wrestler represented India in the 1960 Olympic Games.

In the standing position, a blind wrestler is at somewhat of a disadvantage unless he can hook up with his opponent. Some sighted boys prefer to wrestle in the hooked up position, so there is no problem for a sightless boy. However, others like the open style in which they can go for diving leg tackles. In this case, a blind wrestler must learn to counter as best and as fast as he can. The lack of vision is a handicap in this part of the match. Since most of a match consists of mat, rather than standing wrestling, blind boys are able to demonstrate their abilities in the sport. Here they compete on an equal basis. If the blind wrestler has superior skill, endurance and more knowledge of strategy than does his sighted opponent, he will win.

For a number of years the members of the California School for the Blind wrestling team were guests in the homes of families of the host high school on one or two long trips of the season. These visits proved to be very stimulating and beneficial socially and educationally for both the blind and the seeing boys. A few other schools for the blind, such as Oregon and Kentucky, have made similar trips and overnight stays.

Unfortunately, even today there are some schools and universities that still will not permit blind boys to compete in wrestling. However, Billy Sheridan, "the Knute Rockne of collegiate wrestling," passed away a few years ago without realizing an ambition of his. He had coached the Lehigh University matmen for forty years and was disappointed because he had never had the opportunity to coach a blind wrestler.

Everyone who has had contact with a blind boy before and after he has wrestled interscholastically realizes that the sport has made possible a new outlook on life for him. (See Chapter 14.) Wrestling gives a blind boy confidence because he can win without being given any favors or concessions. Perhaps many blind boys do not know that most sighted wrestlers work harder to defeat them than other opponents.

Swimming

Because of the carry-over value into family and community life, swimming is particularly important for blind boys and girls. Swimming is very definitely a social asset which enables a blind individual to fit into a party at the beach, lake or pool. It is usually somewhat more difficult to teach sightless boys and girls the various strokes, diving and life saving, but a little added patience on the part of the teacher will be rewarded with success.[2] Some may question the practicality of teaching life saving to blind swimmers, but there should be no doubt about it. Blind individuals have rescued others from drowning in deep water.

2. BELENKY, ROBERT: *Swimming Program for Blind Children.* New York, American Foundation for the Blind, 1955, 44 pp.

A sightless person may keep his direction better by swimming beside a wall of the pool. A loud-playing radio is often placed on shore by blind swimmers before they enter a stream or lake. This enables them to locate the shore when they wish to return.

About four fifths of the schools for the blind offering swimming programs use some type of achievement scale. The Red Cross Outline is by far the most commonly used plan. A number of the schools offer opportunities to pass the Boy Scout merit badges for swimming and life saving.

Here are a few activities that have proved valuable in classes for blind swimmers. Some relays that are fun to swim are balloon, candle, umbrella, change pants and auto tube. In the latter event, students sit on top of the tube and paddle. For many years the writer has emphasized the Boy Scout philosophy of relaxation in the water by requiring students to swim as easily as possible on the back for five minutes. Younger children can be motivated to become used to the water by competing with one another in picking up rubber horse shoes from the bottom of the pool. Synchronized swimming for visually handicapped girls should not be overlooked.

Recently, a number of schools for the blind have introduced distance swimming as an important part of the aquatic program. Students of the Oregon School for the Blind swam the 56 miles from Camp Magruder to Astoria by swimming laps in the school pool. Thirteen lengths constituted a tenth of a mile. The distance covered by each student was posted each week. When the total reached 56 miles, a celebration was held. At the California School for the Blind, the older boys' marks in swimming are largely based upon distance swimming. To receive an "A" for the day, a junior high school boy must swim sixteen laps in the school pool, a distance of 640 yds. Standards have been set for different age groups. This motivation has eliminated much "horse play."

In competition, a visually handicapped swimmer is apt to be slowed down somewhat by coming into contact with lane ropes. Lack of vision makes it difficult to perform good turns. A blind swimmer is sometimes defeated in a close race because he cannot see when to make a lunge for the finish line. In back stroke races, someone should be assigned to each blind swimmer to protect the head from striking the wall of the pool on the turns. In a recent swimming meet with sighted boys, totally blind boys placed first in the 50-yd free style, second and third in the 50-yd back stroke and second and third in the 100-yd breast stroke. They were also part of the winning medley relay team.

Blind children participate in a number of water sports with sighted companions. Surfing, water cycling, and water skiing are all enjoyed by some blind youngsters. Skin and scuba diving are among the activities of Camp Lighthouse in New Jersey. A group of visually handicapped water skiers performed every day during the 1953 National Water Skiing Championships at Long Beach, California, and won the hearts of skiers and spectators alike.

Rowing

In England rowing is more common among the blind than in this country. Due to the expensive equipment, the sport has not become popular with American schools for the blind. A crew has been developed by the New York Institute for the Education of the Blind[3] for the past fifteen years or so. Each spring it races four or five sighted crews. The only aid they use is an ordinary thumbtack which is inserted in each oar handle so the oarsman can tell how to properly feather the oar. Most of the competition has been in four-man crew, but some eight-man crew races have been held. In addition partially seeing boys have won sculling races from time to time. Some races have been held in paired-oared gigs. Of course, much practice precedes the racing season. The boys must be taught to keep time, follow instructions, to feather, leg drive, body angle, to secure locks and other rudiments of competitive rowing. They are also taught to avoid catching crabs, skying, washing out and knifing. Some of the schools have summer camps where the boys and girls learn to row. Whether for pleasure or competition, the sport offers the blind little handicap and many advantages.

More consideration should be given to rowing in the education of visually handicapped children. Rowing provides excellent exercise, employing almost all the muscles of the body. It is especially good for developing leg and back muscles. In addition to the

3. HORDINES, JOHN: Competitive Rowing for Blind Boys. *International Journal for the Education of the Blind*, March, 1955, pp. 58-61.

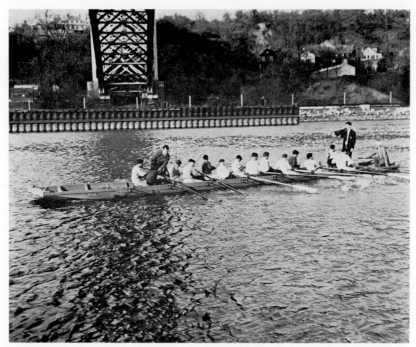

FIGURE 6. Practice for competitive rowing at the New York Institute for the Education of the Blind.

actual physical exercise obtained, rowing is of great value to the blind in general orientation. The boys become acquainted with the boat house and move about freely learning to handle a boat and maneuvering it with grace and skill. One of the most valuable contributions that rowing offers to the blind students is the opportunity to socialize with boys from prep schools and high schools. It is an idealistic sport and is one of the few team sports suited to blind people. Since 55,000,000 people are participating in boating in one form or another today, this is a very good way for visually handicapped youngsters to join the throng, and at the same time, become physically fit.

Bowling

Today one third of the residential schools compete in the National Bowling League of Schools for the Blind,[4] which carries on

---

4. V. R. Carter, Secretary, School for the Blind, Muskogee, Oklahoma.

competition by mail. There are three divisions, Open, Girls' and Junior, in which a total of thirty teams and more than 165 blind bowlers compete. It is hoped visually handicapped bowlers in public schools will also join the league. One of the requirements is that each team has at least two totally blind members. In doubles competition one member must be sightless. A number of residential schools which are not league members carry on an active program of bowling. Schools which do not have lanes on the campus make provision for bowling at a local establishment. Because of the carry-over value into family and adult life, many more visually handicapped boys and girls should be bowling.

In high school, a number of sightless bowlers have averages over 100, while a score of 256 has been bowled by two totally blind men. A blind bowler can take his portable rail[5] and bowl in any lane, regardless of his average. Most of us bowl with handicaps based upon our averages, anyway.

In 1951 The American Blind Bowling Association, P.O. Box 537, Williamsport, Pennsylvania 17704 was organized with four leagues and one hundred visually handicapped adults. Today there are 1400 individuals in seventy-seven leagues, most of them located east of the Mississippi River. An annual tournament is held, and in the 1965 event 164 five-man teams entered. Playing rules in general follow those of the American Bowling Congress. The American Blind Bowling Association awards silver medals to blind and partially seeing male bowlers for scores of 200 and 230 respectively. Similar awards are made to female bowlers for scores of 160 and 180. Bronze medals are given for scores of 190 and 220 for men, and 150 and 170 for women. In general, partially sighted bowlers average thirty pins more than sightless individuals. To encourage participation by public school children, a Junior Division for visually handicapped boys and girls was recently organized by the Association.

Besides the league activity in bowling, a great many visually handicapped people visit local lanes with their families and friends. Here they participate in an activity which can benefit them in health and also socially. The latter point cannot be stressed strong-

---

5. American Foundation for the Blind, New York 11, New York. The cost is $16.30.

ly enough. Let's join the 34,000,000 people who participate in bowling.

Hiking

In hiking a sightless individual takes the hand or grasps the elbow of his companion. Other than this, there is no modification needed. Hiking offers many advantages to all participants, whether sighted or blind. The walking provides vigorous exercise in the fresh air and sunshine. It is generally agreed that there is no better way to build healthy bodies. A love and knowledge of the outdoors can be developed. Hikers are apt to become interested in the conservation of the countryside and keep it free of litter. They will want to learn more about plants and animals. In addition to receiving verbal descriptions, visually handicapped boys and girls should be encouraged to explore by touch wherever possible. Sounds and odors should also be identified. All children like hikes that bring them near a stream, lake or the sea. Blind youngsters are no exception and love to wade and throw stones into the water.

All hikers, including those who are visually handicapped, take pride in their accomplishments, whether it be walking a few miles or climbing a mountain peak. The cost involved is little or nothing, and one needs only one other person to safely participate.

There are some advantages of hiking that are peculiar to blind individuals or of more importance to them. Those activities into which a blind individual can easily fit are highly desirable. Certainly hiking is one such activity. As one hikes along, he will converse and become acquainted with his companion. Such opportunities should not be passed up by those who are visually handicapped. If sightless people are to be accepted in groups of seeing people, they must have something interesting to offer. One has something of interest to talk about with his family and friends after a hike. Another important outcome of hiking for blind people is the marked improvement of walking habits. Since walking habits are poor in many cases, this is an important consideration. Many sightless children have an undue fear of moving about. Hiking can do much to overcome such fear. Improvement in orientation and mobility usually results when a blind individual does much hiking. Where there is no traffic, some totally blind people walk by themselves along dirt roads or well-defined trails, and thus their ability to use environmental cues is developed.

For twenty years there has been a hiking program at the California School for the Blind. There are two parts to the program. The first is a weekly hike which is included in the curriculum of the boys' physical education classes above the third grade. The second part of the program is a voluntary Saturday hike, in which 80 to 90 per cent of the boys and girls participate. Many volunteers from the community act as hiking partners for sightless children. Therefore, the only cost to the school has been the bus driver's fee. Groups of eight students have been transported to Yosemite and Lassen National Parks, where they took challenging hikes, learning much at the parks and on their journeys. Such experiences as these are never forgotten by the children and are invaluable to them in incalcuable ways.

Gymnastics

Exercises on the parallel bars, horizontal bars, horses, rings, etc. have long been a part of the physical education program in many schools for the blind where some fine gymnasts have been developed. Some blind boys compete on high school and university gymnastic teams. A little more time is usually required to teach stunts to the blind students.

Many schools for the blind give annual gymnastic exhibitions. The primary purpose is to educate the public regarding activities of the visually handicapped. The holding of these exhibitions is commendable only when the preparation time is limited so as not to interfere with other physical education activities. In some schools about one third of the school year is devoted to preparation for an event in which only the talented will perform. The author has prepared several satisfactory programs with three or four weeks of concentrated practice. Pupils are then free to engage in a variety of other athletics.

Tumbling

In a difficult tumbling routine one often performs more feats of sheer skill and courage than are required of players in other sports in a whole game. The body control, agility and muscular development which result from tumbling can be used in most games and sports as well as in everyday activities. Lack of vision is not a serious handicap in tumbling. It only makes the teaching of the sport somewhat more difficult.

For the past fifteen years a group of tumblers from the California School for the Blind has performed before 15,000 to 25,000 spectators a year—usually between halves of university basketball games. They have also made several television appearances. In recent years girls were added to the team. Through the appearances of this group, hundreds of thousands of people of the general public have learned of the capabilities in physical activities of blind individuals.

It is desirable to motivate pupils to practice tumbling after school hours so that less class time will be used for this activity. This can be done by setting up badge tests. Some class time is devoted to showing students how to do the stunts and later passing them for awards. Since this is individual work, much can be accomplished informally in the few minutes each day as the class assembles. As soon as a few of the boys and girls start wearing their badges, the program takes care of itself. When a tumbling exhibition is requested, the pupils already have a store of stunts that can easily be worked into a routine. (The badge tests used by the writer will be found in Appendix J.)

Rebound Tumbling

Whatever the age of the participating individual, six or sixty, rebound tumbling is a great deal of fun. Every beginner gets a thrill out of the "big bounce" he experiences for the first time, while the veteran enjoys performing the stunts over and over again. There is much joy derived from springing high into the air and landing on the knees, seat, back and front and then gracefully bouncing to an upright position without any discomfort. Needless to say, most of the muscles of the body are used. Since one must keep his body straight to bounce up and down in the center of the trampoline, this activity usually results in marked improvement of posture of visually handicapped children.[6] The fact that this is a relaxing

6. LOWERY, SHARENE: Rebound tumbling for the visually handicapped. *International Journal for the Education of the Blind,* December, 1960, pp. 44-48.

activity tends to overcome the tenseness found in many sightless boys and girls.

Of course, the use of the trampoline must be very closely supervised with competent spotters present. Noises of other children in the gymnasium must be kept at a minimum so that a blind performer can hear instructions and locate the sound of the bell which is usually attached under the center of the trampoline. For the first few lessons, a safety belt should be placed around the waist of the performer. With an overhead mechanical safety belt,[7] sightless students can be taught forward and backward somersaults. The more complicated stunts, such as somersaults with twists, the Barani, etc., are usually not taught to sightless boys, but it may be possible to teach them to some very talented performers. Otherwise, a teacher of the visually handicapped will usually follow the lesson plan used for boys and girls who have normal vision.

Most physical educators of the blind feel that rebound tumbling is a worthwhile activity for visually handicapped children. However, not all of these teachers feel that the activity can be safely carried on in class time by a single adult. Since the sport is highly individualized, it is not suitable for large classes, such as are found in some schools for the blind. Rebound tumbling can only be successfully carried on with a large group if a second adult is available to supervise the students who are not actively spotting or trampolining. These students should be engaged in some other activity while waiting their turn on the trampoline.

Medicine Ball Hockey

On a 30 x 30 ft. mat, medicine ball hockey is played at Perkins School for the Blind in Boston. Two teams of eight to ten boys line up at opposite sides of the mat. Each team is given a large medicine ball which it tries to roll through the opposing team's defense. A goal is scored when the ball rolls onto the floor behind the defenders. Players may stand or kneel, but the ball cannot be thrown in the air. For this infraction players are sent to the penalty box.

---

7. HORDINES, JOHN: Trampolining for children at the New York Institute for the Education of the Blind. *International Journal for the Education of the Blind,* September, 1953, pp. 200-203.

Volley Newcomb

This game appeals to junior and senior high school visually handicapped boys and girls. It is a good game to cultivate the ability to throw and catch. The totally blind players should do all the serving. A net 7 ft high is stretched across the center of the court measuring 25 x 50 ft. A volleyball or basketball is thrown from behind the end line. The ball is caught by a partially seeing player who throws it back over the net. Play continues until a score is made. One point is scored each time the ball drops to the floor in the opponents' court or it hits the net or is thrown outside the court. Only the serving side scores, and it continues to serve until it loses. Fifteen points constitute a game.

Giant Volleyball

At the New York Institute boys and girls enjoy giant volleyball. The ball is a large Navy rescue balloon with small bells attached to the air intake. While the ball is in flight, the bells jingle. A metronome is placed below the net as a direction finder.

A regulation volleyball court is used, but some of the rules of the game are modified. Totally blind players need only to touch the ball in order to make a fair play when it is served to their side. However, the blind player must make a definite physical effort to touch the ball, otherwise the opposing team is given one point. Other rules may be obtained from the school.

Boxing

The art of self-defense appeals to some visually handicapped boys. Sightless boys are at a distinct disadvantage in boxing. Those with delicate eye conditions should not box. For example, a boy with progressive myopia may lose his vision if a shock should detach the retina. Those with artificial eyes must remove them. If proper precautions are taken, boxing can be a valuable extra-curricular activity for some students. When a sightless boy is boxing, it is desirable to tie a five-foot rope between the opponents.

Kick Over

Kick over is played by two, three or four teams at the New York School for the Blind in Batavia. Each team is given a football and members must kick in order. A player kicks as far as he can in any way that is easiest for him. Teams start at one goal line on a football field and advance to the other end. All members of a team advance or retreat to where the ball stops rolling after having been kicked. A second player kicks, and so on. The team which reaches the far goal line in the fewest number of kicks is awarded 6 points. If two or three teams tie, the 6 points are divided among them.

Dunbar Ball

Dunbar ball is played at Perkins School for the Blind. A rubber playground ball is used. It holds the interest of the boys in the middle grades because each one is an important team member in a fast moving game.

Team A lines up against a gym wall and tries to stop the ball as it is hit to them. A player must always remain in contact with the wall.

Team B stands about 40 ft away. Each boy comes to bat in order. A batter bounces the ball on the floor and swings his fist. Only one swing is allowed. If the ball hits the wall untouched, two points are scored. Any ball hit in "fair" territory, scores one point. When each member of Team B has batted once, the teams exchange places. The game proceeds in innings, similar to baseball.

Goal Ball

A soccer ball with bells in it is used for goal ball, which is best played in a gymnasium or on a tennis court. Two teams scatter about at each end of the playing area. The object of the game is to kick the ball so that it strikes the wall or fence behind the opposing team. In regular order the players place the ball on the ground and kick it back and forth. A kick is made from the point where the defensive player stops the ball. When a totally blind boy kicks the ball, it must be fielded by a sightless defensive player. By kicking the ball on the ground, it usually remains low in flight, thus making it easier for the blind and partially sighted players to field it. The game can also be played with a plastic plate instead of a ball.

A variation is to roll, rather than kick the ball. In Arkansas[8] this game is played by rolling a partially deflated volleyball which tends to hug the ground. There it is called slam ball.

Plate Hockey

Regular hockey is played with a plastic plate and brooms. Each player is given a broom with a stick, 14 in. shorter than is normally used. The shorter stick eliminates injuries from poking. A goal is scored anywhere along the end fence. A tennis court is a good place to play this type of hockey.

Ice Hockey and Other Winter Sports

The pupils of the New York Institute for the Blind play ice hockey in the following manner. Except for a puck made from a flattened gallon can, regulation playing area and rules are used. Behind one goal a student beats a musical cymbal, while a bell is rung at the opposite goal. The coach shouts instructions to the players as the game progresses. There are many spills and the usual rough play.

Other winter sports for blind individuals need little or no modification other than the reduction of speed in some cases. Skiing, ice skating, sledding, snow shoeing, toboggan sliding and saucer sliding are enjoyed just as much by visually handicapped youngsters as they are by those who have normal vision.

Weight Training

It is desirable for visually handicapped people to participate in those activities which need little or no adaptation for them. Weight training is certainly one of these. Practically all of the schools for the blind require the boys on the wrestling team to do some weight lifting of one type or another. It is surprising that so little competitive weight lifting has been carried on interscholastically. Many of these schools also use isometric exercises and ropes to good advantage.

8. HARTMAN, R. E.: A game for totally blind boys. *International Journal of Education of the Blind*, May, 1958, pp. 138-139.

Baton Twirling

Some visually handicapped girls have become quite adept at baton twirling. It usually takes them longer to learn the activity, but many interesting routines have been developed. Some years ago a few girls of the Colorado School for the Blind became so skilled in baton twirling that they appeared in the Pikes Peak Rodeo Parade and also in the State Twirling Championship Tournament.

Golf and Archery

A few schools for the blind sponsor programs in golf and archery, mostly to help acquaint students with these sports. In most cases this information will be used for conversation with seeing persons, rather than participating in the sports. However, there will also be participation by a limited number of visually handicapped people.

Until a few years ago a national tournament was held for blind golfers in which twelve to fifteen participated. The winning scores in the tournaments from 1953 to 1964 usually fluctuated from 204 to 214 for thirty-six holes. At each tournament the blind golfer brings along a sighted golf coach who has practiced with him. The coach gives the approximate yardage and knows what club is needed for a particular shot. The sightless golfer's club head is placed behind the golf ball by his coach. The blind golfer then draws his club backwards and then makes his swing. When the sightless golfer shoots between 100 and 104 for eighteen holes, he is duplicating the par of 72 for sighted golfers. Several blind golfers have shot scores in the 90's from time to time. Golf is practical for only a limited number of blind individuals. For them it can do a great deal of good both physically and mentally.

Fencing

An activity that can be participated in by both males and females, age six to sixty, is fencing. Some blind people have used the regular equipment, while the California School for the Blind has used a new development of the Safe Fencing Company, 21 Harrison Avenue, Glen Falls, New York. This company produces fiber glass fencing foils with rubber suction cup lips. These foils are entirely safe for use without protective equipment of any kind. Fencing requires a surprising amount of energy, and this develops physical fitness. Participation in the sport also results in agility, grace, speed and coordination of movement. Fencing makes a particular contribution to the visually handicapped in the area of sensory development.[9] This is a sport that will appeal only to a certain number of blind children.

Rifle Shooting

One does not ordinarily think of rifle shooting as an activity for blind people. However, a rifle team consisting of students of the South Dakota School for the Blind shoot twenty-two target rifles at targets, covering a 2-in wide pipe from which a short piercing sound is emitted by means of a tube oscillator. Shooting is done from standing, sitting, kneeling and prone positions. The sport is reported to have given great enjoyment and aided in orientation training.

AN EVALUATION OF SPORTS FOR THE BLIND

The physical education program for visually handicapped children should stress those activities which require little or no modification for participation by blind children. Such activities will enable those with impaired vision to participate in physical activities with sighted youngsters on a normal basis, particularly in public schools. The handicapped chilld in a residential school, if given these skills, would not feel out of place when playing with seeing friends at home. Some of these activities are bowling, tumbling, gymnastics, calisthenics, fitness exercises such as sit-ups and pull-ups, swimming, wrestling, weight training, judo, relays, rhythms and dancing, hiking, roller skating, ice skating and other winter sports, rowing, camping, fishing, water skiing, horseback riding, tandem cycling, water cycling, surfing and shuffleboard. Some physical education programs are not placing enough stress on those activities which have carry-over value into family and adult life. This is an important consideration for all programs, but particularly so for those in which visually handicapped boys and girls are enrolled.

---

9. WAFFA, JOSEPH: Fencing—an aid in rehabilitation. *New Outlook for the Blind,* February, 1963, pp. 39-43.

Chapter 8

ACTIVE GAMES

The impulse to play is universal. Blind children want to express their play impulses just as much as do children who have vision. Special effort is required to insure normal growth and development in handicapped children. A good physical education and recreation program will do as much or more than any other school activity to develop normal personalities. Blind children should be taught to play games participated in by their sighted peers in the family and the community. Many games do not depend on sight. Others may be played by blind children after slight modifications have been made. A collection of such games is presented here.

Play not only helps sightless youngsters overcome fear and helplessness, but it also teaches alertness, courage, and skill. By playing active games, children develop habits of health and freedom of motion. Older boys and girls should be encouraged to organize groups for games and to plan picnics, parties, etc. They should take the initiative and not depend upon their teachers. This will help them gain the self-confidence they need so much. Many of the visually handicapped suffer from introversion and other maladjusted types of personality which make it difficult for them to meet sighted people on an equal social footing—something which must be done before happiness and success in life can be attained.

There are two things that blind children should always remember. First, to make acquaintances and friends, they must take the initiative and not expect the public to come to them. Because many blind people have not learned this, they have a tendency to lead a solitary life. Second, a blind child must learn his games thoroughly and be able to play them well before he will be accepted by other children, who are apt to be impatient with him. By playing games with other boys and girls, visually handicapped children get the feeling of "being in things." This gives them self-confidence, ease and freedom of manner.

PRACTICAL HINTS FOR PLAY LEADERS

First, a teacher must really be interested in the development of visually handicapped children. When selecting games one should look for the following characteristics:

1. Blindfolding one or two players;
2. Sound enabling a sightless child to know exactly what is happening;
3. Different duties for the blind and seeing;
4. Running to a goal that can be easily found by sightless players;
5. Limited playing area such as gymnasium or tennis court;
6. Direct contact as in wrestling;
7. Line or chain formations;
8. The possibility of players pairing up in couples.

A teacher of the blind should remember the following suggestions when planning and conducting physical education and recreation activities.

1. Plan your program in detail. Choose games suitable to the age of the players and make certain that the totally blind can take an active part in the program.
2. Radiate enjoyment and enthusiasm. Players give back the the spirit set by the leader.
3. Understand thoroughly what you want done, and make your directions brief and clear. Demonstrate the action when possible.
4. See that all the children are included in the game.
5. If a game confuses the players, discard it and choose another.
6. Stop a game before it becomes "dead."
7. Keep things moving for the entire play period.
8. Play the game yourself now and then.
9. Always insist on fair play. Teach children that defeat resulting from an honest trial of strength is more honorable than victory gained by cheating.
10. Maintain a general condition of order, but let players

shout all they want during games and relays. Never attempt to explain anything until the class is quiet.

11. Draw boundary lines, obtain necessary equipment, etc., before the beginning of the class period.

12. Encourage timid children to give dares and take reasonable risks.

13. Encourage losing teams so they will not lose heart and give up.

ACTIVITIES TO AID ORIENTATION AND MOBILITY

Training for independence in mobility should begin in early childhood[1] in the home. A child should be encouraged to explore independently. If he grows up in an environment of overprotectiveness and fearfulness, a child's confidence in himself may be so destroyed that he will not learn to travel as independently and as well as a youngster who has been raised in a normal environment. Thus, a blind child's home life determines to a great extent the progress he will make at school in mobility and orientation.

Physical education can contribute much to the development of a child's confidence and independence. In the primary grades rhythm games, running, skipping, jumping and other activities encourage fearless freedom of movement and train the sense of direction. As the child passes through the intermediate grades, he will play many active games, start tumbling and gymnastics, begin to roller skate and participate actively in other sports which will result in improved mobility skills.

In addition to regular games and sports, a physical educator can do much to improve orientation by using specific games and contests. Activities which will overcome the fear of moving about rapidly are very valuable. First, students may run hand in hand with the teacher. Next, a partially sighted student may take the teacher's place. A student then should be taught to run by himself, moving toward a whistle which is being blown. The next step is to run across the gymnasium or small play area by himself.

Jumping often presents a problem. First, encourage the student to jump from one place to another on the floor or ground. Next,

---

1. HETHERINGTON, FRANCIS: Elementary school travel program. *International Journal for the Education of the Blind*, October, 1955, pp. 15-17.

the child should jump from the first step of a stairway. He may then jump from a bench and later from higher objects until he jumps from heights of three or four feet. In the beginning, mats may be used to jump onto, so as to decrease fear. Jumps may be made first by holding the teacher's hand. Next, a seeing student may act as a partner. Finally, the student is encouraged to jump independently.

To overcome the child's fear of the water, the teacher should get into the swimming pool with him, take his hand and walk around the shallow part of the pool to make him aware of the rope which separates the shallow from the deep water. He should be sure to point out to the student that the rope is there for the child's protection to prevent him from unknowingly going into deep water.

A child should be encouraged to learn independent travel to and from the physical education class. In the beginning the instructor will walk with the young children, giving them information as to how they can make the trip by themselves. After a little while more and more independent travel is encouraged. For the first year or two the physical education teacher will observe and give help only when absolutely necessary. By the second or third year a child should be able to travel independently to the gymnasium or play field.

Developing an obstacle sense is very important in avoiding bumps and accidents. One way to start such training is to conduct a contest to see who can walk across the gym and come to a stop closest to the wall without touching it. After children have become adept at doing this, place a blackboard in front of them at some distance. Again students try to walk as close to the blackboard as possible without touching it. The distances should be varied.

A contest which will develop desirable skills is to see who can walk in the straightest line. Another activity is to have the class start at the center of the gym or play area and then scatter. The contest is to determine who can return closest to the starting point.

Children may walk around the asphalt paths on the ball field or around the edge of a large mat in the gym. This can be made into a contest to determine which sightless child can cover the distance in the shortest length of time.

When blind man's buff is played by giving the blind man a bell, the game is markedly improved for sightless players. Players run away from the sound of the bell, and the blind man runs toward the sounds of their shouting or hand clapping.

Bell tag is much improved when played in this manner. Seeing players take turns running about the gym or tennis court, ringing a bell. Sightless players run toward the sound and try to tag the player carrying the bell. When a sightless player has made three such tags, he rests until the end of the game.

A variation of the above game is to have the instructor dribble a basketball about the gym or tennis court. Of course, the area must be free of objects that might cause injury.

Hiking can improve the walking habits and mobility skills of blind children. This has been a result of the active hiking program at the California School for the Blind.

The English electronic ball improves the game of circle numbers. Players sit cross-legged in a circle, and each is given a number. The instructor drops the audible ball in the center of the circle and calls a number. The player with this number rises and picks up the ball as fast as he can. During this action, the leader counts silently one to ten. If the ball is not picked up by the count of ten, one point is counted against the player. Play for about ten minutes. Two champions should be named—the sightless player and the sighted player with the fewest points.

In this activity, which aids orientation, players stand 10 to 15 ft. apart along a wall or fence. The instructor rolls a bell ball to players in turn, from a distance of 30 to 40 ft. Each time the ball is not caught by the player who was called, he is given a point against him. Each round the catching should be made more difficult. Determine two champions, one sightless and one seeing.

Sightless and blindfolded players stand together in the center of the gym. The instructor calls a particular part of the gym by name. The players run to the area. The one reaching it first is the winner. Eliminate the winner each time and play again and again. In this way players with poor orientation skills get most of the practice.

A variation of the above contest is winds. Each wall of the gym is designated as East, South, West and North. Players run to the wall called by the leader. Eliminate the winner and play again and again.

Other activities which are particularly valuable in developing orientation skills are animal chase, belled cat, court ball, wall ball, snatch the bacon and bear, wolf and sheep. For the full description of these games, the index may be consulted for the page number.

In teaching physical education activities, stress should be placed upon the student's knowledge of his position in the room or on the play area, his position in relation to other children, and the position and direction in which he is moving. The child should be made aware of cues which may be helpful to him, such as sounds, direction of the wind and sun, terrain under foot, land marks, etc. Nothing can be more important than to give a sightless child a better understanding of his environment and make it easier to accomplish his goal of being able to travel safely and independently.

GAMES FOR PRIMARY CHILDREN

Only a limited number of games for primary children is included here because the singing games and imitation activities of this group need no adaptation for blind children. The words and music for such games as "Farmer in the Dell," "London Bridge," "Looby Loo," "Mulberry Bush," and "Nuts in May" will be found in Bancroft's *Games*[2] and other books which may be purchased at most book stores.

CLASSIFICATION OF GAMES

The natural interests of a healthy child lead him to care for different types of games at different periods of his development. For this reason the games in this chapter are classified as to age groups. Such a classification is merely suggestive and does not set up any dogmatic limitations.

  (P)   Primary, six to nine years of age.
  (I)   Intermediate, ten to twelve years of age.
  (J)   Juniors, thirteen to fifteen years of age.
  (S)   Seniors, sixteen and over.

---

2. BANCROFT, J.: *Games.* New York, Macmillan, 1946, 685 pp.

Games will be introduced in this manner—animal chase (P. I). This means that the game appeals to children in the primary and intermediate grades.

Only boys should participate in rougher contact games, including those in which one team removes shirts for identification. Chapter 13 lists boys' games and girls' games.

Animal Chase (P, I)

This game is best played on an asphalt court or in a gymnasium about 50 ft. wide. All the players line up along one side, and "it" takes his place in the middle of the playing area. He calls the name of some animal, such as dog, cow, cat, whereupon all the players must run across the playing area, imitating the animal designated. Anyone caught before reaching the opposite side must join hands with "it" and help him catch other players. The one originally "it", remains the caller throughout the game. The last one to be caught is "it" for the next game.

The game can be played by assigning an animal to two or three players. When the name of an animal is called, only those who represent it run across the court.

Ball Tag (I, J)

This game should be played in the gymnasium or on an enclosed area such as a tennis court. Although it is not necessary, blind players may pair up with someone with sight. The players scatter irregularly. One player, who is "it", tries to hit one of the other players with a large utility rubber ball. Any player hit becomes "it" and tries to tag others in the same way. Throws can be made anywhere, but sighted players must advance the ball by dribbling it. This will enable sightless players to locate "it". If "it" is totally blind, he may carry the ball (no dribble necessary) and throw it at other players, located by their shouts, hand clapping and footsteps. Each time a player is hit, one point is counted against him. When a player receives three points against him, he must pay a forfeit. Boys like to line up and have him "go through the mill." The player who paid the forfeit becomes "it" with no points against him, while other players retain their points. A ball rebounding from a wall or fence is "dead."

Battle (J, S)

The teams are stationed at opposite ends of a gymnasium. The members of one team should remove their shirts. At the signal, the teams try to capture opposing players and take them back to their own goal. A captured player may resist as he is being taken to the goal, but once there, he must remain quiet until time is called. The team having the most men at the end of the game, wins.

Battle Ball (I, J, S)

Mats are laid across the gymnasium floor, establishing two throwing lines about 20 ft. apart. Each team is given a medicine ball and takes a position behind its throwing line. The sightless players on each team do the throwing while sighted players field the balls. When a seeing player stops a ball, he hands it to a thrower who tries to hit the opposite wall. Throwers must roll the ball rather than hurl it in the air. Any rolled ball that hits the wall will score.

Bear, Wolf and Sheep (P, I)

Two players are chosen, one to be the bear and one the wolf, and each has his den. The other players, who are sheep, scatter irregularly on a rectangular playing area, shouting, "Baa, baa, baa." At a signal, the wolf and the bear try to catch the sheep, who must not go out of bounds. When a sheep is caught, it is taken by the captor to his den. Sheep must walk to the den and are not permitted to resist. At the end of two minutes, a whistle is blown to stop the game. A count is then made of the sheep that are free and of those in the den of the wolf and the bear. If most of the players are free, the sheep win. If most of the players are in the den of one of the chasing animals, that animal wins. The game may be repeated with another bear and wolf.

Belled Cat (P)

One player, the "cat", carries a bell loosely in one hand, so that it will ring with every step. The other players represent mice and try to catch the cat. The player that tags him becomes the new cat.

Big Black Bear (P)

The playing area for this game can be on the playground or in the gymnasium. A den should be designated for the bear, and blind players should pair up with a seeing peer. Some time is given for the bear to hide. Then the other players set out to seek the bear, chanting "Oh where, oh where is the big black bear?" When the seekers come close to the bear, he dashes out and tries to tag as many runners as possible before they reach home base. The teacher may choose the next bear, or the last person tagged becomes the bear. The game may be repeated.

Birds and Snake (I, J)

This game is best played in the gymnasium or on a rectangular strip of lawn. One team represents the "snake" and lines up along the goal line. The other team acts as "birds" and stands on a line at the opposite end of the playing area. At the signal, the birds attempt to reach the goal line. The snake, moving forward with hands linked, tries to encircle as many of the birds as possible. The birds are not allowed to run out of bounds or go under the hands of their opponents. When the two ends of the snake join, the game halts, and the catch is counted. The two teams then reverse offices and the game is started again. The second catch is counted. The team catching the most birds wins.

Boiler, Boiler, Boiler, Blue (P)

This game can be played in the gymnasium or on the playground. One player is chosen to be the tagger, while the others scatter about the play area. The tagger, clasping his hands in front of him, calls out, "Boiler, boiler, boiler blue, if you're careless, I'll catch you!" He then tries to tag a player with his clasped hands. If successful, they join hands and become partners, repeat the rhyme, and try to tag a third player with their clasped hands. When caught, the third player clasps his own hands, repeats the rhyme in unison with the first two players, and starts chasing other players. The game is continued until all have partners or there is just one player left. The last player to be caught wins the game.

Boiler Burst (P)

Establish a goal line about 30 ft long. All the players except one stand in a semicircle 30 ft from the goal. The extra player stands in the circle and tells a story. At the most exciting moment he says, "And then the boiler burst," whereupon all the players run for the goal. "It" runs after them, attempting to tag one. Any player tagged by "it" before reaching the goal, becomes "it" for the next game.

Bull in the Ring (I, J)

The players stand in a circle with hands firmly grasped, forming a closed ring. One player who is the bull, stands within. The bull tries to break through a pair of clasped hands. If he fails on the first attempt, he is given two more trials. When the bull has broken the ring or failed in three trials, the teacher selects another bull. The game is played until all have had a turn as bull.

Team Bull in the Ring (S)

Two teams stand in separate circles. One player of each team stands in the circle formed by the opposing team. At the signal, each bull attempts to break out of the circle that encloses him. The bull which breaks out first scores one point for his team. Two new bulls are appointed and, at a signal, the game continues. Every player should have the opportunity to act as bull. The team scoring the most points wins. If neither bull breaks out in one minute, the game is halted, no score is made, and two new bulls are appointed.

Call Ball (P)

The players form a circle with one in the center. A ball, preferably one with bells in it, is given to the center player, and he calls the name of one to whom he wishes to roll the ball. If a basketball is used, it should be bounced, rather than rolled. The player whose name is called says, "Here," and the center player rolls or bounces the ball to him. If that player fails to catch it, the center player calls another one to receive the ball. If he catches it, he takes the place of the center player.

Circle Bell Tag (J, S)

All the players but one stand in a circle, and the extra player takes a position outside of the circle. At the signal, the players in the circle pass a cowbell from one to another, attempting to keep the bell away from "it." The bell must always be passed to the next man, either on the left or on the right. Any player responsible for "it" touching the bell must exchange positions with him, and the game continues.

Circle Stride Ball (I, J, S)

All but one of the players form a circle, standing in stride position, with feet touching those of the next player. The odd player stands in the center, and tries to roll a basketball or bell ball between the legs of a player in the circle. The circle players use their hands to prevent the passage of the ball. Play continues until the center player succeeds in sending the ball between some player's legs. The two players exchange places, and the game continues.

Court Ball (I, J, S)

A gymnasium or tennis court is a good playing area for this game. Whenever possible, a soccer ball with bells in it should be used. Divide the group into two teams, the throwers and the runners. The runners line up along one side wall. Along this same wall, and at a distance of 20 ft to 30 ft, one of the opposing players takes his position to be the thrower for the half inning. The other players on the thrower's team line up across from him along the opposite wall. The runners announce the name of the player who will run, and the thrower indicates by name the player to whom he will roll the ball. At the signal "go," the runner runs across the court and back. In the meantime, the thrower rolls the bell ball to his designated player who tries to catch it and throw it back. If the *thrower* catches the ball before the runner makes a round trip, his team gains one point. Otherwise, the *runners* score one point. When all members of the running team have had a turn, the teams exchange positions. In each inning a different player must serve as a team's thrower. The number of innings played will be determined by the number of players. Smaller groups will play more innings, while larger groups can complete fewer innings. It must be remembered that the thrower must throw to a different teammate each time in the half inning.

Club Ball (I, J, S)

Two teams line up 20 ft apart. An Indian club is placed in front of each player. The first player of Team A calls out or claps his hands to indicate his position, and the first player of Team B rolls a basketball or bell ball toward him to knock over his club. If a player's club is knocked down, he is out, and he must take his club and leave the game. A player on Team A tries to hit one of Team B's clubs. The players must roll in turn. The team eliminating all of its opponents first wins.

Crossing No Man's Land (J, S)

This game is best played on a rectangular strip of lawn or in a gymnasium, preferably with a large mat surface. Team A lines up at one end of the playing field, and Team B stands in the center of the field. At the signal, the players of Team A run for the opposite end of the field, shouting and clapping their hands. The players of Team B attempt to prevent them from reaching their goal. Any player of Team A who is forced to touch any part of his body other than his feet to the floor or ground is eliminated. Each player who reaches the opposite end of the field, without running out of bounds, scores one point for Team A. The two teams exchange positions and Team B attempts to make a crossing. The team scoring the most points wins.

Crows and Cranes (I, J)

Two teams stand about three feet apart, facing each other at the center of a gymnasium or tennis court. Base lines are the end fences or walls. One team is designated "crows" and the other "cranes." If the leader calls, "crows," the crows turn and run back to their base line. Any player caught by the cranes must join the captors. If the leader calls, "cranes," these players run in the same manner. The calls of the leader should be drawn out as long as possible by drawling the "r" in "crows" or "cranes." The team having the largest number of players at the close of a given time wins.

Do or Die (J, S)

In separate huddles give two teams exactly opposite instructions. For example, one team is told to leave the gymnasium and the opponents are instructed to stop anyone leaving the room. Of course, a struggle develops around the door which should be left open during the contest. This is a good way to close a physical education period now and then.

Dog Tag (I, J)

One player acts as a post and stands in one place. Another player represents a dog and grasps the free end of a 15-ft rope, held by the post. The other players tantalize the dog by running into his area and shouting. The dog tries to tag one of them, but he must hold one end of the rope. When a player is tagged, he takes the post's position. The post becomes the dog, and the old dog joins the group of runners.

Every Man Tag (I, J)

This game is best played in the gymnasium or on a rectangular strip of lawn. The players stand in the safety zones (gym mats) at either end of the playing area. One player runs into the neutral zone and another player tries to tag him. A third player tries to catch either of these two, and so on. The object of the different players is to make captives of the others, as any player caught must join hands with his captor and try to catch others. As the game continues, the players are gradually gathered into different parties. Players may return to the safety zones at any time. One player may catch only one opponent at a time. The side wins that captures all of the players.

Flowers and the Wind (P)

Divide the players into two groups and assign each group a goal. The goals are about 20 ft apart. One group chooses a flower, and these players approach the goal of the other group, the wind. The players of the wind try to guess the name of the flower. When a guess is correct, the flowers turn and run for their goal and the wind pursues them. Any flower caught must join the wind. Repeat until all the flowers have been caught.

Flying Dutchman (P)

All the players except two join hands in a circle. Two sightless players should not stand next to each other because a player may have to run with either of his neighbors. The two extra players join hands, walk around the outside of the circle, and tag the joined hands of any two players. The pair who were tagged chase the taggers around the circle. Players must keep their hands clasped while running. The object of both pairs of runners is to get back first to the vacant space. One pair succeeds; the other pair becomes runners, and the game continues.

Follow the Leader (P, I)

The players form a column, and one player is appointed leader. The leader performs various stunts, such as climbing over obstacles, jumping certain distances, walking 10 ft with a book on his head, etc. Players who fail to do any stunt set by the leader go to the foot of the line. Only one attempt is allowed at a hazard. The instructor should change leaders after every four or five stunts.

Forcing the City Gates (J)

Two teams line up facing each other about 20 ft apart and holding hands. The captain of the team stands at the left of the line, and his strongest player stands next to him, the weakest player being placed on the right end of the line. One player is named by the captain of Team A to break through Team B's line. If he succeeds, all the players cut off from the captain's end of the line must cross over and join the attackers' side. If the runner fails, he must join the defenders' side. The captain of Team B then selects a runner to try to break through the opponents' line. The side wins which secures all of the opposing players.

Hide and Seek (P)

One player covers his eyes and the others hide. When securely hidden, they call out, and the one who is "it" goes in search of them. When "it" finds the hidden players, the object is won.

Hold the Fort (J, S)

A mat placed at one end of the gymnasium represents a fort. One team is designated "defenders," the other "attackers." At a signal, the attackers try to force their way into the fort; the defenders attempt to throw them out. All tactics are fair except unnecessary roughness. Time is called at the end of two minutes.

Each attacker in the fort scores one point for his team. The two teams reverse positions, and the game is repeated. The players in the fort are counted for the second time. The team with the highest score at the end of the game wins. If any part of a player's body touches the floor outside the fort, he is considered out. It is wise to have the boys on one team remove their shirts.

Horses and Riders (I, J)

Two captains agree on boundaries and select a goal. One team, representing the riders, stands at the goal, and the players cover their eyes. The horses scatter and hide, sightless players pairing up with partially seeing players. After counting to 100 by ones, the riders start out for the chase, leaving one of their number to guard the goal. If a horse tags the goal without being tagged by a rider, he scores one point for his team. Horses that are tagged before they reach the goal are considered caught. The game continues until all the horses are caught or reach the goal. The two teams then exchange offices and the game is repeated. The team with the most horses safely reaching the goal wins.

Last Couple Out (J, S)

All the players except one form a column of couples, sightless players pairing up with sighted children. The extra player, who is the catcher, stands about ten feet in front of the first couple with his back to them. The catcher calls, "Last couple out!" Then the last couple in the line separates and runs forward, one on the right side of the double line, and the other on the left side. They try to join hands in front of the catcher before he can tag either of them. If a player is tagged, he becomes catcher. The old catcher joins hands with the other player and they take their places at the head of the line. If a couple succeeds in clasping hands, they take their places at the head of the line, and the catcher calls again, "Last couple out!"

Line Blind Swat (J)

All the players but one stand in line holding hands. The extra player is blindfolded and given a swatter. From a position 20 ft in front of the line, he runs after the other players, attempting to swat one of them. The line may run anywhere, but must retain its formation of grasped hands. Any player hit becomes "it," and the game continues.

Medicine Ball Wrestle

Two teams of equal strength are chosen. To make identification easier, one team removes its shirts. The objective of each team is to make it possible for one of its members to stand up with the ball overhead. To win, some strategy must be used, so instructions are given in a huddle. One boy is chosen to handle the ball, while the others are assigned certain opponents to drag away from the ball. The strategy is similar to a play in football.

All dangerous tactics such as striking, scratching, pinching, etc., are forbidden. Wrestling holds are limited to those used in the amateur sport. The physical condition of the boys should determine the length of the contests.

In one variation of team medicine ball wrestling the objective is different, but the strategy and rules are the same. One team tries to take the ball from a large mat to the floor, while the op-

FIGURE 7. Medicine ball wrestle.

ponents try to keep it on. If the offensive team has not gained its objective in two minutes, their opponents take a turn trying to push the ball off the mat. The offensive team with the shortest elapsed time wins.

In still another variation the game is started in the middle of a wrestling mat. Each team attempts to carry the ball over the opposing team's goal line, which is the edge of the mat. Push ball, using a large cage ball, is played in the same manner. In all of these variations it is important that members of one team remove their shirts.

Midnight (P)

An enclosed area such as a gymnasium or tennis court is a good place to play midnight. All the players stand in a semicircle with the fox in the center. The players ask, "What time is it, Mr. Fox?" If he replies that it is any hour except midnight, they remain standing. When the fox shouts "Midnight!" the players run to the far fence or wall. The fox follows the sound of the footsteps and tags a player. This player becomes the next fox, and the game is repeated.

Mouse Trap (P)

A small circle of three to five players is formed. The other players stand in line holding hands. They march through the circle until the teacher says, "Snap!" The circle players quickly shut the trap by dropping their clasped hands. Some of the mice will be caught and must join the circle, making the trap larger. The game continues until all the mice are caught.

Novelty Progress (I)

All the players line up at one end of the playing area. The first player moves across the playing field in any way he may choose. The second player may move in any way except that used by the first player. Each player must choose a method different from any used by his predecessors. The game continues until all have crossed the playing field.

The Ocean is Stormy (P)

This game is best played in a gymnasium or on a tennis court.

One of the end walls or fences is designated as home base. All players form couples, clasp hands, select a name of a fish and scatter about. The extra pair, known as sharks, walks around the area, calling the names of fish. When the name of a fish which has been adopted by a couple is called, that pair falls in behind the sharks and marches after them. When the sharks have called all the fish they can think of, they say, "The ocean is stormy," whereupon all the players run for home base. Hands must remain clasped throughout the game. The last couple to reach home base becomes the sharks for the next game.

Partner Tag (I)

All the players clasp hands in couples. One pair is "it" and tries to tag other couples. Any pair tagged becomes "it." However, the player tagged must place his left hand on the spot touched, whether it be his head, back, foot, etc. In this position the pair attempts to tag other couples. When they succeed, the "poisoned" player is relieved from his position.

Pinch-o (I)

All the players but one stand in a line and hold hands, facing the goal line 30 ft in front of them. The extra player stands 10 ft in back of the line. The player on one end of the line calls, "Pinch!" and squeezes the hand of the player standing next to him. In this manner the pressure is passed from player to player until it reaches the other end of the line. When the last player feels the pressure, he calls "O!" Then the players in the line, clasping hands, run to the goal line. Any player tagged by "it" must join him, and the game continues until all but one have been caught; he is "it" for the next game.

Rattle Snake (J)

All but three of the players join hands in a circle. One player, who is the snake, is given a can with a pebble in it. Two other players, representing hunters, are blindfolded. The three players stand inside the circle. One of the hunters calls, "Rattle snake" whereupon the snake rattles the can. The hunters attempt to catch the snake who must respond to every request to rattle. When the snake is caught, he joins the circle of players, and the hunter who caught him becomes snake. A new hunter is appointed and the game continues.

Round-Up (J)

All but four of the players scatter over a limited playing area, such as a tennis court. The four players, representing the round-up crew, join hands and chase the other players who are steers. To be captured, steers must be encircled by the round-up crew; the two end players joining hands. Captured steers withdraw to one side of the playing area. When four steers have been caught, they join hands and become the round-up crew. The old round-up crew become steers and the game continues. Steers are permitted to break through the hands of the round-up crew.

Run, Sheep, Run (I, J)

Sightless players pair up with partially seeing players in this team game of hide and seek. While one team faces the wall, the captain of the other team is hiding his players. He returns to the goal and accompanies the searching team. Using a code, he calls out signals to his men, enabling them to approach nearer the goal without being seen or heard. Neither team may run for the goal until one of the captains shouts, "Run, sheep, run!" A captain will give this signal when he thinks his team can reach the goal first. If all the sheep reach the goal first, they win and hide again. If all the searchers reach the goal first, they hide for the next game.

Sardines (P, I)

One player hides while the rest count to 100. When the counting is finished, they set out to hunt. Any player discovering the hider crowds into the hiding place. Soon the players are packed in like sardines. If there is not room to hide in the same place, the finder sits down near the hiding place. When the last hunter discovers the spot, the game starts over, the first finder becoming the hider.

Slap Tag (P, I)

Two teams line up facing each other at least 30 ft apart. The hands of Team A are extended, palms up. A player from Team

B comes forward and goes down the line touching each hand. Finally, he slaps a hand and runs back to his own line. The player whose hand was slapped, chases him. If the runner is tagged, he joins Team A. The chaser then taps the extended hands of Team B. The side having the largest number of players after five minutes of play wins the game.

Smuggling the Booty (J)

Team A stands at one end of the gymnasium while the players of Team B remove their shirts and take a position in the center of the playing area. Some small object (booty) that can be carried in the pocket is given to Team A, and a player is secretly selected to carry it. When the leader calls, "Smugglers," Team A runs forward trying to draw attention to a player who does not have the booty. Team B attempts to catch them; to be caught a player must be thrown to the floor. Caught players withdraw to one side. The game continues until the player with the booty is caught or reaches the opposite wall safely. The teams exchange positions for the next game.

Stone (I)

A small mat (5x7 ft) is placed at one end of the gymnasium. The wall at the far end is the goal line. One player, the stone, sits on the mat while the other players stand around the outside of the mat. They taunt the stone by shouting and stepping over into his territory. Finally, he shouts, "Stone!" whereupon all the players run for the goal. The stone quickly rises and chases them. Any player tagged must join the stone sitting on the mat. They also join him in chasing the other players whenever he gives the signal. This continues until all the players have been caught.

Tie the Prisoner (J, S)

Two teams each stand in a circle and select a prisoner. Each prisoner steps into the opponent's circle. Give each team two pieces of rope 6 ft long. At a signal, both teams catch the prisoner in their midst and tie his hands and feet as quickly as possible. Unnecessary roughness is forbidden. The team which ties its prisoner first wins.

Tommy Tiddler's Ground (P)

A space, known as Tommy Tiddler's ground, is designated. Tommy Tiddler stands in this area. The other players run into the territory saying, "I am on Tommy Tiddler's ground digging gold and silver." If any player is tagged while in Tommy's territory, that one becomes Tommy Tiddler.

Treasure Smuggling (I)

Select a base on the playground or in the gymnasium. Boundaries are mentioned beyond which no player is allowed. Players are divided into two groups, the smugglers and the cops. The treasure, which is something small, is given to a member of the smugglers' group. His identity should not be known to the cops. Sightless players in either group pair up with a seeing playmate. The smugglers are given an opportunity to hide. At the end of a reasonable period of time, the teacher gives a signal to the cops to start the search. In the meantime the smugglers try to reach the base without being tagged. When a cop tags a smuggler, he says, "Pony-up the swag!" If the smuggler does not have the treasure, he goes free and the hunt continues. If, when challenged, the smuggler has the treasure, he must deliver it to the cops and shouts, "Ship ahoy!" whereupon all remaining smugglers must race for the base. The cops win the game and become the smugglers for the new game. If the holder of the treasure can return to the base without being caught, his side wins and takes another turn as smugglers.

Wall Ball (J, S)

This game is played in a gymnasium. Two teams are chosen and one of them, Team A, scatters about the gym. A member of Team B stands 10 ft from the end wall and throws a basketball or bell ball against the wall, so it will not strike at a height of more than 6 ft. As the ball bounces towards the other end of the gym, members of Team A attempt to catch it. If the ball strikes the far end of the gym without being caught, a point is scored by Team B. All of the players take a turn in throwing the ball against the wall. Then Team A takes its half inning to attempt to score. The team with the most points at the end of seven innings is the winner.

SUMMARY

The games described in this chapter will suggest many others that have not been included. The games presented here were chosen with three thoughts in mind. First, games should be suitable for groups whose members have varying degrees of vision. Second, the sightless players should have an equal opportunity to win each game. Third, games must be active and interesting. It is a popular belief that blindness forces a boy or girl to be inactive. However, it is obvious from the wide variety of games presented here that this need not be the case.

Chapter 9

CONTESTS

MANY THINGS CAN BE SAID in favor of devoting a physical education period every two weeks to contests. First, this type of exercise provides excellent all-around training. Second, it is an established fact that contests develop qualities of self-confidence and aggressiveness. Third, any number of children over ten years of age may take part in this activity. When in doubt about the grade level of a contest, refer to Chapter 13 for suggestions. Fourth, blindness is no handicap in the contests presented here. Fifth, this type of exercise has carry-over values for afterschool hours because many of the activities require only one or two competitors.

NOVELTY RACES

There are many novelty races in which the blind child can compete on an equal basis with his seeing peers. When sightless entries are in a race, the instructor or a student should run a few yards in front of the contestant, blowing his whistle. This is better than standing at the finish line because it enables a blind child to run in a straighter line. Races should be held some distance from trees, poles and other obstructions. If possible, the finish line should be some familiar boundary, such as the edge of a lawn or an asphalt surface.

Many of the relays described in Chapter 10 are based primarily on locomotion. Since the method of running is the same in the individual race as in the relay, there is no need to repeat them here.

Children eliminated in contests which continue to progress should be assigned such temporary activities as rope jumping. The contests in which it is suggested that shirts be removed by one team should be limited to male players. Only boys should be permitted to participate in the rougher contact contests. In certain contests, such as rodeo racing, the instructor should be sure that weights are more or less equalized. If the skill is complicated and dangerous, speed should be removed and only accuracy emphasized.

Cat-Tail Chase

Players stand abreast in line and the center man acts as a pivot. The players on either side of the pivot represent a team. One team faces about. Then all the players of both teams join hands, inside players of both teams linking hands with the pivot man. Retaining their hand grasps, both teams run forward in a circle about the pivot. The race continues until the outside player of one team tags the outside player of the opposing team. If a team breaks, its opponents win the race.

Centipede Overtake Race

Set some chairs in a circle around which teams must run. The circle should not be more than 30 ft in diameter. Divide the group into two teams which are stationed on opposite sides of the circle. The members of each team line up in file formation, each file headed by a leader with some sight. Each player holds the waist of the player in front of him. At the signal they run, attempting to tag the other team. If the line breaks, the team must stop at once and rejoin its parts.

Chariot Race

Three players constitute a chariot. Two represent horses while the third as driver. The horses join inside hands and the driver places a piece of cord or broomsticks in their outside hands. At the signal, the driver, who has some sight, drives his horses to the finish line.

Chinaman's Race

A team consists of three players and lines up in file formation. Each of the first two players reaches back between his legs with his right hand and grasps the left hand of the player in back of him. In this position they race to the finish line.

Crawling Race

Players get down on all fours and at a signal, race on their hands and knees to the finish line.

Paper Race

Give each player two folded newspapers. Cardboard or flat wooden blocks may be used. The runner places one of the papers on the ground for each step, as it is a miss for the foot to rest on anything but paper.

Quartet Race

A team of four players lines up facing the starting line. The players stand abreast and join hands. At the signal, they race to the finish line 30 to 50 yd in front of them. Any team failing to keep hands clasped is eliminated.

Rail Riding Race

A team of five players straddles a long pole. The players facing front grasp the pole with both hands. They run to the finish line while straddling the pole.

Rodeo Race

A team consists of three players. The first player stands on the starting line. The second player stands behind him, bends down and grasps him around the waist. The third player jumps on the second player's back, and the three race to the finish line.

Trio Race

Give each team of three players a broomstick. The players, using both hands, hold the broomstick across the front of their chests and run forward to the finish line.

MASS CONTESTS

Basket Team Goal

Divide the group into two teams with an equal number of sightless players on each team. Give each team a basketball and assign it a goal. The captains number their players consecutively, and the members of the team must shoot in turn. The seeing players shoot for the goal from the free-throw line, while the blind players may stand closer. At the signal, the two Number one's shoot for the basket. Anyone on the team may catch the ball and pass it to the Number two player who tries to score. Each time a basket is made, the entire team shouts, "One," "Two," "Three," etc. The team which scores 25 points first, wins.

Battle of Knights

This event should be played on a turf to eliminate danger from falls. Players compete in pairs, a horse and rider. The riders mount the horses' backs. At the signal, the pairs try to upset each other. The rider may use his hands to push and pull, and the horse may charge. The pair wins that remains standing when all others are down.

Blind Walk

Establish a starting line and place a ball 90 ft in front of it. The first player stands on the starting line and is blindfolded. He spins around three times on the starting line, and stands still. A player standing near the ball, blows his whistle once or twice. The blindfolded player takes thirty steps in the direction of the sound and the ball. His thirtieth step is marked, and he removes the blind. The other players repeat the procedure. The player whose thirtieth step is closest to the ball wins.

Catch and Pull

A line is drawn across the middle of the playing area. Two teams line up facing each other. The game consists of pulling opponents across the line in any manner that is not unnecessarily rough. When a boy has been pulled entirely over the line, he must help his captors. The team wins which has the most players at the end of two minutes.

Champ Rest

An idea which may be used to advantage in conducting races and contests is to rest the winner. Run a short race and eliminate the winner. The same race is run again and again, each time eliminating the winner. The weaker contestants, those who need development, get most of the exercise. Don't overlook such champ rest contests as these: (a) jumping from a ledge (not more than 3 ft in height) and climbing back up to stand erect; and (b) jumping for distance from a low ledge.

Elbow Tug-of-War

A line of players stands abreast midway between two base lines, which are ten feet apart. The players count off by two's. All the two's then face about in the opposite direction, and all of the players link elbows. At the signal, each team attempts to pull its opponents across the base line in front of it.

Four-Way Tug

The ends of a rope are tied together so that it makes a circle about 5 ft in diameter. The rope is placed in the center of a large mat, and four boys grasp it at different points. At the signal, each contestant tries to pull so that he can touch the floor on his side of the mat. Eliminate the winner and play again.

King of the Mat

Any number of boys kneel on the floor around a large square mat. At the signal they rush to the center of the mat. Each boy tries to make an opponent touch the floor by pushing him off the mat. As soon as a boy touches the floor, he must leave the mat. The struggle continues until one boy becomes king of the mat.

If additional contests are held during the same period, do not permit winners to take part. This gives weaker boys more exercise and the thrill of winning.

Team King of the Mat

Divide the group into two teams of equal numbers. The members of one team remove their shirts so that both teams can be easily distinguished. Each team takes a position on the mat and at a signal tries to push its opponents off the mat. Any player forced to touch the wooden floor is eliminated and must withdraw. The contest continues until one team is completely eliminated.

Last Man Over

Establish two lines 50 ft apart. The players line up along one of the lines. At the signal all run for the opposite line. The last man over is eliminated and must withdraw from the field of play. Players may not intentionally interfere with an opponent. Before each signal is given, the instructor should announce that the players are to hop across, double jump across, run across on all fours, and so on. The elimination continues until all but one player has been forced to withdraw.

Line Push

Two teams face each other, standing shoulder to shoulder in the middle of a large mat. The players of each team link arms and move forward so that the two teams stand chest against chest. At the signal, each team tries to push the other back over the edge of the mat. The contest continues until one team is pushed entirely off the mat.

Low Bridge Elimination

The players line up in a column. Two players stand in front of the line and hold a short stick at the height of the chin of the tallest boy or girl. Each player in turn tries to pass under the bar with hands on hips and bending backwards; the knees may be bent. Those who fail to make the passage, drop out of the line. Each time the bar is lowered 2 in and players may be forced to drop out. This continues until a champion is determined.

Mat Scramble

A small mat 5 x 7 ft is placed in the middle of the gymnasium, and the group is divided into two teams. The players of one team remove their shirts so that both teams can be easily distinguished. The two teams line up at opposite walls and, at a signal, rush forward. The players of each team attempt to get on the mat and at the same time throw opposing players off. The team having the most players on the mat at the end of a two-minute period, wins. A player is not considered to be on the mat if any part of his body is touching the floor.

Poison Snake

The players form a circle and grasp a rope, the ends of which have been tied together. The "snake" takes his place in the center of the circle, carrying a whistle or Halloween noise-maker. At the signal, the "snake" makes noise and the circle of players revolves, forcing a child to touch the "snake". Any player letting go of the rope or touching the "snake" is eliminated, and the contest is continued until a winner is determined.

Rope Jumping

All of the children in the class find partners. One child counts while the other jumps rope. At the end of a one-minute period, players exchange positions. The jumping may be free-style, or certain methods may be specified. Boys in good physical condition may be permitted to find the player who can jump the most without missing. There is no time limit for such a contest.

Simon Says

The players stand facing the leader. The teacher says, "Simon says, 'Squat!' " whereupon he squats. The players must all do likewise. From time to time the leader makes a movement, omitting the words "Simon says," saying, for example, "Reach for the sky". In this case any player imitating the teacher is eliminated. The contest is continued until a champion is determined.

Stalking

A lawn or a large mat surface in a gymnasium is a good place to hold a stalking contest. Players kneel along one edge of the area and crawl on hands and knees. The instructor stands 30 to 40 ft in front of the players, but facing away from them. The teacher begins to sing or blow a whistle and the players advance toward him. When the instructor wills, he stops singing and turns around quickly. If he sees any player moving, that player is called by name and must return to the starting line and begin again. The leader faces away from the players, sings again, stops, turns around and looks for moving players. The contest continues in this manner until some player crawls across the finish line. This player is the winner. Eliminate the champion and play again.

Stunt Elimination

To add interest, make available stilts, hula hoops, pogo sticks, gymnastic apparatus, etc. The first player in line performs some stunt which most of the players can do. The instructor should decide whether a stunt may be used. The players who fail to perform a stunt are eliminated. After all of the players have made an attempt, the first man falls in at the foot of the column. The second man then sets a stunt and players may be eliminated again. This continues until all but one have dropped out; this player is the winner.

Tug-of-War

A long rope is stretched out on a level surface; one team lines up at one end, the other team at the opposite end of the rope. A center line is marked, and the players grasp the rope. At the signal, the tug-of-war begins. It is won when all of the members of one team have been pulled over the center line.

A variation is to have players of each team pair up as horses and riders. The riders mount the horses' backs and hold the rope. At the signal, the teams pull. Any rider falling must let go of the rope until he is mounted again.

Weather Vane

The group stands in open formation, and the instructor takes his place in front of the players. The leaders calls the various points of the compass—north, south, northeast, etc. After each command, players quickly face in the direction ordered. Any player who faces in the wrong direction is eliminated. The last player to be eliminated is the winner. Older boys and girls may be required to face the opposite direction from that which is called.

INDIVIDUAL COMBATIVES

In physical education classes one of the best ways to conduct individual combative contests is by the team line method. The players of each team are numbered consecutively, so that contestants with the same number stand opposite each other. The weakest player on the team should be assigned Number one and the strongest boy represents the highest number. The two Number one's come forward, and engage in the contest set by the instructor. The winner earns one point for his team. The two's repeat the contest, and one of the teams is awarded a point. This continues until all the players have competed. The team winning the greatest number of contests, wins the meet. Several contests may be carried on in a half-hour program.

Arm Lock Wrestle

Two players sit on the floor, back to back, spread their legs widely, and lock arms at the elbows. Each boy tries to lean to the left, endeavoring to pull the other over, so that his right arm or hand will touch the floor.

Back to Back Lift

Two opponents stand back to back with elbows locked. By pulling and bending forward, each contestant attempts to lift the other off the floor.

Back to Back Push

Two players take a position in the middle of a mat and stand back to back with elbows linked. Each boy pushes backwards, attempting to push the other over the edge of the mat. One may not lift and carry his opponent.

Back to Back Stick Pull

Two opponents stand back to back, and hold a broomstick high overhead. Each performer tries to pull the stick forward and out of the grasp of his opponent.

Ball Wrestle

Two boys put their hands on a medicine ball, placed in the middle of a mat. Each contestant attempts to take the ball away from the other, using only fair tactics. This is accomplished when no part of the opponent's body touches the ball. Another contest is to take the ball over the edge of the mat behind the opponent.

Boundary Tug

Two players face each other in the middle of the mat, right toes touching, and each stepping back in a strong stride position with the left foot. Both players grasp a short broomstick, and each tries to pull the other over the edge of the mat.

Bulldog Pull

Place two small mats together, establishing a boundary line. Two players get on their hands and knees, facing each other, and a strap is placed around their heads. At the signal, each tries to pull the other over the boundary line between the two mats or force him to lower his head so that the strap will slip off.

Chinese Tug

Two players stand back to back on either side of a line. Each boy bends down and reaches back between his legs with his right hand and grasps the other's right hand. At the signal, they attempt to pull each other over the line.

Hand Wrestle

Two boys face each other, grasp right hands, and place the outer edges of their feet together. They brace themselves by putting their left feet back. At the signal, each player tries to throw the other out of balance. The left hand must not be used against the opponent. As soon as either foot is moved, a fall is counted.

Hand Push

Two players stand with their toes touching, facing each other. They raise both hands and place them against the palms of the opponent on a level with the shoulders. At the signal, each pushes the other's hands until one is forced to step back.

Hoop Tug

The ends of a rope are tied, making a hoop 2 ft in diameter. Two boys stand back to back and slip the hoop down over their heads to the level of the waist. They take a position midway between two lines 15 ft apart. At the signal, each attempts to pull the other over the line.

Indian Wrestle

Two players lie side by side on their backs with their heads in opposite directions. They hook right elbows. The referee counts "One," and the players raise their right legs and touch them to together. At the count "Two" this is repeated. At "Three" the right knees are hooked and each contestant tries to turn the other over backward.

Leg Tug-of-War

Each boy wraps a towel around his right ankle and then ties one end of the 3-ft long rope tightly over the towel. The contestants face away from each other and move apart until the rope is taut. A line is made under the middle of the rope. At the signal, each, while hopping on the free foot, tries to pull the other over the line.

Lifting Contest

Two boys stand facing each other with chests touching. Each contestant places his left arm over the opponent's shoulder and his right arm about the opponent's waist and clasps hands behind the opponent's back. Each boy tries to lift the other off the ground. After the signal to start has been given, the original hold may be broken.

Neck Pull

Two players stand facing each other, bend forward with heads up and clasp each other around the neck with both hands. Each contestant tries to pull the other forward 6 ft.

One Man Pull

In the middle of the mat two boys stand facing each other. They grasp each other's wrists with both hands and try to pull the opponent over the edge of the mat.

Pull Over

Mark two lines 15 ft apart. Two players take a position midway between the lines, standing back to back. They grasp each other's wrists with a wrist grip. Each contestant tries to pull his opponent over the line.

Push Over

In the middle of the mat two players face each other and place their hands on the opponent's shoulders. By straight pushing, each contestant tries to push the other back over the edge of the mat.

Stick Pull

Two contestants sit on the ground, each having the soles of his feet pressed against those of his opponent. The players grasp a broomstick and hold it crosswise above their toes. Each tries to pull the other to a standing position. A player releasing the stick loses.

Stick Turn

Two players face each other, extend their arms overhead and grasp a broomstick. At the signal, they step backward and slowly draw the broomstick down between them, each trying to retain his own grip and make the stick turn in his opponent's hands.

Stork Wrestle

Two contestants clasp right hands and stand on their right feet. By pulling and pushing with the clasped hand (body-bucking is not allowed), each contestant tries to force his opponent to fall over or touch his raised foot to the ground.

Tractor Pull

Place two small mats together, establishing a boundary line. Two pairs compete at one time. Two players represent horses and take positions on hands and knees, facing in opposite directions. The other players face in the same direction as their horses. They mount the horses' backs, wrapping their legs around the horses' bodies. The players then reach back and grasp each other's wrists. At the signal, each pair attempts to pull the other over the boundary line. If a rider falls, his opponents win the contest.

Two Stick Wrestle

Two sections of broomstick, each about 1 ft. in length, should be made available. Two opponents face each other, and each player grasps each stick. The object is to wrest one stick out of the grasp of the opponent.

SUMMARY

Contests suitable for blind children usually have one of these features: (a) players are in contact with each other; and (b) contestants compete in pairs or groups. The second arrangement makes it possible for a sightless player to team up with a sighted boy or girl.

Chapter 10

TWENTY SELECTED RELAYS

R ELAYS CAN MAKE a definite contribution to the physical education program. This activity can be conducted almost anywhere, even indoors during inclement weather. Much fun and healthful exercises are provided by relays. Blind children can fit easily into many relays, especially the twenty selected for presentation here. These relays will certainly suggest many others.

When a skill is complicated, children should have an opportunity to practice it before it is performed in a relay. For blind children it is desirable to establish a turning point which can easily be recognized by them. Outdoor relays are best set up with a turning line at the edge of a lawn or asphalt surface. Indoor relays can be run on a mat surface 5 ft wide and 20 ft long. One mat surface should be provided for each team. Outdoors, and sometimes indoors, the instructor should stand near the turning line and blow a whistle. As a blind performer returns from the turning point, teammates should shout to give him direction. Blind children will easily fit into relays conducted in this manner.

Here are some activities which may be used as races or relays: (a) crawling backwards on all fours; (b) couples running, clasping inside hands; (c) couples running with inside legs tied together, three-legged; and (d) jumping in sacks. The lame dog race or relay should not be overlooked. The locomotion in this activity is on both hands and one foot, while holding the other foot out behind and off the floor.

Bicycle Tire Relay

At the signal, the first and second players stand close together and slip an old bicycle tire (a rope with ends tied may be used) down over their heads and around their waists. They run to the turning point and back and then remove the tire so that the third and fourth players may repeat.

Caterpillar Relay

The first two players face each other and get astride a stick 4 ft long which is held with both hands, one hand in front and the other in back. In this position, they run to the turning point, one traveling forward and the other backward. At the turning line they reverse direction and return so that the next couple can repeat.

Centipede Relay

The first two members of a team place a stick between their legs, holding it with one hand and both face forward. They run to the turning line and back, giving the stick to the next couple.

Chain Relay

The second player bends down and grasps the first player by the ankles. In this position, they move to the turning line and return, touching off the next pair who repeat.

Dirty Sock Relay

All team members stand astride in a column. At the signal, the last player bends down and crawls between the legs of his team-mates. When he reaches the front of the column, the player stands up and shouts, "Dirty sock!" This is the signal for the last child in the column to repeat the action. When all players have taken a turn, the relay is completed.

Donkey Relay

The second player leaps on the first player's back. They race to the turning line, where they reverse positions and race back to the starting line, touching off the next pair.

Dressing Relay

This description is for girls, but the relay could be adapted for boys. Teams in play clothes line up behind their captains. One girl stands 20 ft in front of her team. Each captain is given a brassiere, pair of panties, slip, blouse and skirt. At the signal, each captain races to the girl facing her team. The girl standing in front can call teammates. Upon reaching the standing girl, the captain gives her the articles of clothing to hold. Then the captain puts on each article of clothing. When dressed, she runs around the standing girl and removes the clothing. She then takes the clothing back to the second member of her team. Each girl on the team repeats the routine.

Jump Stick Relay

Two players hold the ends of a stick, one on each side of the column. Holding the stick close to the ground, they run to the end of the column and return. Each player in the column jumps over the stick as it comes to him. The first pair gives the stick to the third and fourth players and goes to the far end of the column. The team arriving in its original position first, wins.

Leapfrog Relay

Each player leans forward placing his hands on his knees in leapfrog position. At the signal, the rear player vaults over all the players in turn. Upon reaching the front of the column, he shouts, "Leapfrog!" This is a signal for the last child to repeat the action. The team arriving in its original position first, wins.

Military Relay

The first player passes the ball over his head to the next player, and it is thus passed to the rear player. When the rear participant receives the ball, he shouts, "About face," and the ball is passed between the legs to the head of the line. The front player commands, "Right face," and the ball is passed sideways down the line. The rear player shouts, "About face," and the ball is passed behind the back to the front man to finish.

Pass Through Hoop Relay

An old tire tube or a hoop 3 ft. in diameter may be used. At the signal, the first player carries the hoop to the turning line and slips it over his body, head first. He steps out of the hoop, and carries it back to the next player. The routine is repeated by each player.

Raised Leg Relay

The first player stands on one foot and raises the other backward so that it may be grasped by the second player. In this position, they move forward to the turning line. Here the positions are reversed and the players return, touching off the next pair.

Rope Skip Relay

The first player of each team skips rope in place ten times. The rope is then passed to the second player who repeats. This continues until all have skipped the required number of times.

Rope Obstacle Relay

The first player is given a common ruler or a piece of rope one ft. long which he holds with both hands. At the signal, he steps forward over the rope (still holding it with both hands) and passes it to the second player, who repeats and so on to the end of the line. After stepping forward over the rope, the rear man steps back over it. The rope is then passed to the person in front of him, who steps back over it and passes it up the line. After stepping back over the rope, the front man should hold it taut overhead to indicate his team is finished.

Sedan Relay

The first two players join inside hands and a light player is selected to be "king". At the signal, the "king" sits on the joined hands of the first pair, placing his arms around their shoulders. He is carried to the turning point and back to the starting line. Each pair in the column gives the "king" a ride, and the contest ends when all have run.

Siamese Twins Relay

The first two players on each team stand back to back and straddle a broomstick, grasping it with both hands in front. At the signal, they move toward the turning line, one running forward and the other backward. Upon reaching the turning line, they stop, and without turning around, return to the starting line. The broomstick is given to the next pair, who repeat.

Snake Relay

The first player reaches back between his legs, with his left hand and grasps the right hand of the second player. In this position, they run to the turning point and return to the starting line, touching off the next pair, who repeats.

Stride Relay

At the signal, the first player passes a basketball between his knees to the player behind him and so on down the line. As soon as the last player receives the ball, he crawls forward under the column of players to the front of the line and passes the ball as before. The team returning to its original position first, wins.

Tandem Relay

The second player circles the front player's waist with his arms and clasps his hands. In this position they run to the turning point and back to the starting line, touching off the next pair who repeats.

Wheelbarrow Relay

The first person in each couple (the wheelbarrow) walks on his hands, knees stiff, legs extended and back straight. His partner grasps his knees. At the signal they move in this position to the turning line. Here they reverse positions and return, touching off the next pair.

SUMMARY

A good program of relays must have intelligent leadership and placement of players. The best method is to place teams in parallel columns. Captains should not let blind players represent consecutive numbers on the team. A helpful practice to determine winners is to have each player sit on the floor upon finishing. Always give encouragement to the losing team.

Chapter 11
THE PHYSICAL FITNESS OF BLIND CHILDREN

W ITHIN THE PAST TEN YEARS there has been a tremendous growth in the concern for the physical fitness of our people, particularly youth. This concern arose from the discovery that children in many other countries of the world were much more physically fit than American boys and girls. As a result, physical fitness programs are being stressed in more public schools than ever before. The program most widely used is the Youth Fitness Test[1] developed by the American Association of Health, Physical Education and Recreation. This test has been adopted by the President's Council on Physical Fitness. Under the leadership of President John F. Kennedy, the Council became a strong force in developing physical fitness programs throughout the United States. In addition, other valuable programs of physical fitness have been developed, such as the California Physical Performance Tests[2] and the Physical Fitness and Proficiency Test of the Amateur Athletic Union.[3]

These are valid tests which will determine pupils' physical abilities. By using the tests, a teacher can determine which pupils are below average in physical fitness. When a pupil has been identified as being physically undeveloped, the teacher should do extra work with him to improve his physical capacity. A regular testing program will accurately measure the progress made by pupils in developing physical fitness.

In the most widely used tests, certain items are not valid for blind youth. In order to bring information on the physical fitness

1. *AAHPER Youth Fitness Test Manual. American* Association of Health, Physical Education and Recreation, 1201 Sixteenth Street, N.W., Washington 6, D. C., 1965. Price $1.00.
2. *California Physical Performance Tests.* California State Department of Education, 1962, 109 pp. Sacramento, California.
3. *AAU Physical Fitness and Proficiency Test.* Available free of charge from the Amateur Athletic Union, 231 West 58th Street, New York, New York.

of blind children up to a par with that of children with normal vision, some studies were conducted. Valid standards for visually handicapped boys and girls were determined.

STUDIES OF THE PHYSICAL FITNESS OF BLIND YOUTH

The writer has conducted a number of studies on the physical fitness of visually handicapped children. In one study, Motor Performance of Visually Handicapped Children,[4] one fifth of all children over ten years of age in schools and classes for the blind participated.

During the school year 1961-62, the AAHPER Youth Fitness Test was administered to 1400 students in eighteen residential schools for the blind and five public school classes.[5] The survey was organized by Charles R. Young, Athletic Director of the Texas School for the Blind.

Much valuable information has been obtained from the results of the various studies on physical fitness of visually handicapped children conducted over a period of twenty years. Test results indicate the performance of blind youngsters is equal to that of sighted children in pull-ups, sit-ups, squat-thrusts and standing broad jump. Visually handicapped children perform far below the average in the 50-yd dash and the 600-yd run. The weakest event for sightless children is throwing, particularly a softball. These weaknesses in running and throwing are probably due to the fact that sight plays an important role in learning and performing these skills. For example, those with partial vision run faster and throw farther than do those who are totally blind. However, they do not perform as well in these events as do sighted children. Youngsters who lose their vision after six years of age run and throw much better than do those who lose their vision early in life. So obviously, standards must be set up for the sightless in running and throwing events, and another set must be established for those who have partial vision.

The mean scores in running and throwing for older pupils in

4. BUELL CHARLES: *Motor Performance of Visually Handicapped Children.* Ann Arbor, Michigan, Edwards Brothers, 1950, 125 pp. Summarized in *Journal of Exceptional Children,* December, 1950, pp. 69-72.
5. Panel Discussion. Physical Fitness, the President's Council and the Physical Education Workshop Survey. *Proceedings American Association of Instructors of the Blind,* 1962, pp. 50-58.

schools for the blind more nearly approach the norms for the seeing than do scores of younger visually handicapped children. This would indicate that blind girls and boys make good progress in the ability to use their muscles during their school years. Boys with defective vision perform relatively better than do girls. One reason for this is that special schools usually provide more physical education for the male sex.

In running, jumping and throwing, overprotected blind and partially seeing boys and girls perform far below the norms of other blind children. The attitude of parental overprotection very definitely influences the performance of any event in the physical fitness tests.

When the writer administered the Iowa Brace Test, which is a stunt type of test, many of the same conclusions mentioned above were reached. For example, partially seeing children perform relatively better than do sightless pupils. On all levels of the Iowa Brace Test, the scores of the partially seeing fall consistently below those of seeing children.

It is generally understood that throwing for distance for sighted children, when done in correct form, is a test that has the highest correlation to excellent physical performance. However, since effecting the proper form for throwing in blind children is so time consuming on the part of the very busy teacher, and the benefits gained can also be gained by doing other exercises, it has been decided by many physical educators of blind children that the event should not be included in testing for physical fitness. This does not mean to imply that one throwing event should not be continued to be used in interscholastic track meets for blind children. If throwing is to be used, there is no agreement as to whether it is better for blind children to throw the softball or basketball. About one half of all the physical educators of visually handicapped pupils favors throwing a basketball, while the other half likes the softball throw for distance better. Another point to be brought out here is that there is no great concern about the weakness of blind boys and girls in throwing for distance because sightless people have very little occasion to use such a skill.

Poor performances of visually handicapped pupils in running is of great concern, however. Running is a measure of a very important aspect of physical fitness, so physical educators of blind children should work diligently to improve the child's performance in this event.

WHY USE ADAPTED TESTS?

There has been some reluctance on the part of some physical educators of the blind to recommend and accept physical fitness tests adapted for visually handicapped children. From a questionnaire it was learned that practically all of the physical educators in schools for the blind favored adapting physical fitness tests, while some teachers in the public schools felt no modification was necessary. Those who opposed adaptation of tests were unable to offer any commonly used test that would be fair to blind children.

The Army or Navy Tests might be used for boys, but there is no provision for girls. Even in these tests some of the events are not used for visually handicapped children. Some states have fitness tests, but most of these must be modified or scaled differently for blind children, and the averages apply only to one state. For example, averages are high in California due to the daily physical education requirement and the fact that the weather permits more outdoor exercise. There are a few tests that might not need modification, but they take much time or expense to administer. These tests are impractical and not widely used.

The great majority of physical educators of blind children favor adapting either the AAU or AAHPER Physical Fitness Tests, which are the most widely used tests in public schools. More of these physical educators like the AAHPER Test, but there are quite a number who feel both tests should be adapted. Upon obtaining this information, the writer undertook the task of adapting these tests for use with blind children.

Adaptation of AAU Physical Fitness Test

Most of the events in the AAU Physical Fitness and Proficiency Test need no modification when used for visually handicapped children. The 50-yd dash must be modified to be fair. However, one set of standards for blind children and another set for partially seeing pupils have been established. Surprisingly enough, in the other running event, the one for distance, the standards for seeing children are also fair to blind pupils. For some girls and younger boys, some slight modifications in the standing broad jump standards were made. Since these modifications are slight, some groups of blind children can use the regular scale for the standing broad jump. In the other required events, walk and run, sit-ups and pull-ups, no modifications are required for use with visually handicapped children. In addition, the contestant must select one event from push-ups, running high jump, continuous hike for distance and softball throw. A sightless boy or girl could choose either the push-up event or the continuous hiking for distance. Of course, the hiking would be done with a sighted partner. The standards in push-ups and hiking are fair, both for the sighted and the visually handicapped.

The modifications mentioned above have been approved in writing by the AAU Headquarters. In fact, copies of the modified test are available free of charge from the organization. It should be stressed that the AAU is anxious to award certificates to visually handicapped boys and girls who pass the tests. These certificates will be the same as those awarded to sighted children. Visually handicapped children can be proud of earning the certificates, because they will be awarded only to those who qualify.

When testing visually handicapped boys and girls, the regular scales should be used, except for the modification listed below.

FIFTY-YARD DASH FOR VISUALLY HANDICAPPED BOYS AND GIRLS
TIME IN SECONDS

	Blind Boys	Partially Seeing Boys	Blind Girls	Partially Seeing Girls
Age 6-7	13	11.0	15	13.0
Age 8-9	12	10.0	14	12.0
Age 10-11	11	9.0	13	11.0
Age 12-13	10	8.5	12	10.0
Age 14-15	9	8.0	11	9.5
Age 16-17	8	7.5	11	9.5

STANDING BROAD JUMP
FOR VISUALLY HANDICAPPED BOYS AND GIRLS

	Boys	Girls
Age 6-7	2 ft	2 ft
Age 8-9	3 ft	3 ft
Age 10-11	4 ft	3 ft 6 in
Age 12-13	5 ft	4 ft
Age 14-15	6 ft	4 ft 6 in
Age 16-17	7 ft	4 ft 6 in

Perhaps some explanation of running for blind children should be made. If guide wires are available, they should be used both for the dash and the distance run. In the latter event, a boy or girl would run back and forth the required distance. If guide wires are not available, a sighted student may run 10 or 15 yds in front of a totally blind runner blowing a whistle or shouting. The blind runner will follow the sound. This method can be used in the dash, but in the walk-run a blind runner may grasp the hand or elbow of a sighted student. The partners then run the required distance.

Adaptation of the AAHPER Physical Fitness Test

The seven events in the AAHPER Physical Fitness Test are pull-ups, sit-ups, standing broad jump, 50 yd dash, 600 yd run, shuttle run and softball throw. The norms for blind and seeing children are the same for pull-ups, sit-ups and standing broad jump. However, modifications must be made in the other four events. As suggested above, it is best to eliminate the throwing event for visually handicapped children. If the physical educator wishes to include throwing, it is suggested that Buell's achievement scales for the basketball throw be used. Achievement scales for visually handicapped boys and girls in the 50-yd dash, 600-yd run and the shuttle run will be found in Chapter 12. It will be noted that there are separate standards for the blind and partially seeing in these three events.

To fairly administer the AAHPER Physical Fitness Test, the regular norms are used in pull-ups, sit-ups and standing broad jump, while Buell's achievement scales are used as standards in the 50-yd dash, 600-yd run and the shuttle run. Since the shuttle run must be so markedly modified, physical educators may wish to use Buell's achievement scale for squat-thrusts instead. The latter event has the advantage that it is based on the same norms as those of the seeing.

The AAHPER Headquarters has given permission to award certificates and chevrons to visually handicapped boys and girls, using the adaptations mentioned here. To receive a merit rating, each event must be passed at the 80th percentile or higher. To receive a standard rating, each event must be passed at the 50th percentile or higher.

The California Alternate Minimum Physical Performance Test

In California a minimum physical performance test has been developed which may be used as *one* measure of a pupil's progress. In addition, skill tests, rating scales, check lists, etc., should be used. This new test (1965) should be of interest to physical educators of blind children because no modification of events is required for visually handicapped pupils in Grades 4 through 8, and only one high school event, the 600-yd run, must be scaled differently. The test at each grade level consists of three events, basically pull-ups for boys and knee push-ups for girls, knee bent sit-ups and standing broad jump, except that the high school students run instead of jump. This test can be obtained from the California State Department of Education, Sacramento, California.

SUMMARY

It is important for each one of us to exercise vigorously for thirty minutes each day. It is highly desirable that our schools measure the physical fitness of children and work with them to improve their physical capacities. The President's Council on Youth Fitness[6] has made many helpful suggestions for a school-centered youth physical fitness program.

Only necessary adaptations of two widely used physical fitness tests have been made for use with visually handicapped children. Both the Amateur Athletic Union and the American Association of Health, Physical Education and Recreation are anxious to award regular certificates and chevrons to blind children when these modifications are used. Visually handicapped children can be proud of these certificates because the difficulty for passing the tests has been equalized for both groups.

---

6. *Youth Physical Fitness.* President's Council on Youth Fitness, 1961. For sale by Superintendent of Documents, U. S. Government Printing Office, Washington 25, D. C. Price $.40.

Chapter 12

PHYSICAL EDUCATION ACHIEVEMENT SCALES FOR VISUALLY HANDICAPPED BOYS AND GIRLS

As time passes, our schools are making more and more use of objective measurements. Thus, our procedures are based more and more on a scientific basis, rather than individual experience and opinion. Standardized measurements in physical education of blind children were made available by Buell[1] almost twenty years ago in the form of achievement scales. Using much new information, these scales have been revised where necessary and are presented in this chapter. These new standards are based upon thousands of performance records collected by the writer. In addition, results of the testing program of the American Association of Instructors of the Blind,[2] in which 1400 children participated, were used. Except for the shuttle run, each achievement scale is based upon at least 500 performances, and in some cases, 2500 performances. These figures may not appear to be particularly large, but it must be remembered that the number of blind children is not large. Since they are widely scattered, a testing program of any size involves a great deal of effort.

Due to the fact that blind children are so widely separated, a teacher without a standardized measuring device finds it almost impossible to accurately evaluate performances of individuals or groups. The scales presented here may be used to good advantage for such evaluations. These evaluations should be made at least once a year. Objective measurement is just as essential in physical education as in any other subject.

---

1. BUELL, CHARLES: *Sports for the Blind.* New York, American Foundation for the Blind, 1947, 240 pp.
2. Panel Discussion. Physical Fitness, the President's Council and the Physical Education Workshop Survey. *Proceedings American Association of Instructors of the Blind,* 1962, pp. 50-58.

PURPOSES OF ACHIEVEMENT SCALES

In constructing achievement scales, percentiles are used. Since scales have been constructed in a number of events, it is possible to objectively rate a student in a variety of skills and performances. If he makes a score of 80, he is excellent, a score of 50 rates him average, and below 30 indicates weakness in the event. If a weakness is identified, a program of correction should ensue. In the same way, the physical educator can rate his program. He may find it strong in running events and weak in developing arm strength, as shown by tests in pull-ups and rope climb. The teacher could then reorganize his program to overcome any weakness found.

A student is interested in knowing whether he is above or below average in various physical performances. Besides comparing his records with those of other students, a child is interested in comparing his performance with previous efforts. Thus, a testing program can make teaching more meaningful, both to the student and the teacher. Results of achievement scales will motivate most boys and girls to practice during and after school hours to improve their performance records and overcome weaknesses. A rating of a child's physical performance should become a part of his permanent record in the administration office.

By establishing norms, competition can be held among students of dissimilar ages and amounts of vision. Decathlons and pentathlons, based upon achievement scales, will motivate nearly every pupil to improve himself in physical skills and performance. As mentioned in Chapter 11, selected scales may be combined into a valid physical fitness test. For such a purpose one might use the scales for sit-ups, pull-ups, standing broad jump, 50-yd dash, 600-yd run and possibly either squat-thrusts or shuttle run.

Some of the important components of physical fitness are arm and shoulder strength and endurance, abdominal strength, leg power and strength, flexibility of legs and body, speed, cardiovascular endurance, agility, strength, coordination and body control. Pull-ups for boys and knee push-ups for girls measure strength and endurance of the arm and shoulder girdle, while sit-ups evaluate abdominal strength. The knee bent sit-ups have been used in California because experimentation and analysis have shown that this exercise is a better measure of abdominal strength and endurance than sit-ups with legs straight. The standing broad jump assesses power, strength and flexibility of legs, and the physical fitness component measured by the 50-yd dash is speed. A good test of cardiovascular strength and endurance is the 600-yd run-walk. The common measure of body agility, coordination and control for seeing children is the softball throw, which is not a valid measure for visually handicapped boys and girls. A better measure of this component in blind children would be ten-second squat-thrusts. The shuttle run, because of several variables, may be difficult to administer by inexperienced persons, particularly for visually handicapped pupils. If the shuttle run is used, it will evaluate speed and agility. For sightless children, it will also indicate the development of the perception of direction, which is so important in moving and traveling around. Of course, such perception is not commonly thought of in physical fitness testing, but it nevertheless is most important for those who are totally blind.

Fortunately, a good measure of physical fitness can be obtained by giving four or five performance tests. A test should be selected to measure each important component of physical fitness. An instructor should take care not to duplicate tests for a single component.

DEVELOPMENT OF STRENGTH AND MOTOR SKILLS

In order to accurately evaluate the growth of strength and motor skills, one must know the relative importance of various factors in such development. About thirty years ago, Neilson and Cozens[3] developed classification systems using height, weight and age. Thus, the advantage of size in physical performance was nullified.

In 1950, Buell[4] found that the classification of visually handicapped children differed in some respects from that used by Neilson and Cozens for seeing children. Buell found that weight had less influence on the performance of blind children than it did on the performance of boys and girls with normal vision. He also found that height of children with visual impairments was not as

3. NEILSON, N. P. AND COZENS, F. W.: *Achievement Scales in Physical Education Activities for Boys and Girls in Elementary and Junior High Schools.* New York, A. S. Barnes, 1939, p. 162.
4. BUELL, CHARLES: *Motor Performance of Visually Handicapped Children.* Ann Arbor, Michigan, Edwards Brothers, 1950, p. 73.

important in motor performance on the high school level as it was for seeing children. Using partial and multiple correlation techniques to solve four-variable problems (age, height, weight and performance), best-fit classification indexes were developed. From these indexes, classification charts were constructed.

Recent research, using many thousands of children in public schools, has been summarized by Espenschade[5] in these words: "The use of age alone as a basis for the development of test norms is recommended. Although a combination of age, height and weight has a somewhat higher predictive value than age alone in a few tests at several age levels for boys, the amount of improvement is not sufficient to justify the labor involved." It has been found that the child who is taller and heavier than others of the same age cannot always be expected to perform better. One reason for this is that children of certain races, such as Orientals, perform as well as do individuals of other races who are taller and heavier. So most norms today are given according to age and sex only. In some cases, even these norms should be interpreted. Whether an individual can ever be "average" or "superior" will depend upon factors peculiar to him. One factor which must be taken into account, particularly for visually handicapped children, is home environment. Mention has already been made of the poor motor performance of blind children who are overprotected by their parents. Another factor to be considered is the amount of previous practice in motor skills which varies markedly from child to child. Research clearly shows that those who have had more practice perform better.

Several studies have shown that the development of physical abilities is much more closely related to skeletal, rather than to chronological, age. A valid measurement of skeletal age can be obtained from x-rays of the hand and wrist. These studies have found that a wide range of maturity exists among children of the same sex and same chronological age. A recent report[6] on Little League baseball players (boys eight to twelve years of age) showed

---

5. ESPENSCHADE, ANNA S., Restudy of relationships between physical performances of school children and age, height, and weight. *Research Quarterly,* May, 1963, pp. 144-153.
6. KROGMAN, W. M.: Maturation age of 55 boys in the Little League World Series, 1957. *Research Quarterly,* March, 1959, pp. 54-56.

the great majority of the players on the championship teams were advanced two or three years in skeletal age.

The meaning of norms should be understood by teachers, children and parents. Regardless of where a child is on the scale, he can be expected to improve with age. If he is at the 30th percentile in Class E, he should ordinarily attain this level in Class D. If he attains a higher level in Class D, this is a gain over and above what is to be expected from growth. A child who performs at the 50th percentile is average, while one who reaches the 80th percentile is outstanding in his performance.

CLASSIFICATION

From the above information, it would appear desirable to classify children according to skeletal age. Since this classification is impractical in normal school routine, it will not be used here. Height and weight will not be used because it is likely that these factors are no more important in motor skill development than are home environment, practice and other conditions. Thus, it would appear that a useful classification system can be based on chronological age alone. When performance is poor for an individual, the teacher should take into account such factors as overweight, overprotection and amount of practice when interpreting norms.

CLASSIFICATION BY AGE

Boys		Girls	
Age	Class	Age	Class
17 and up	A	16 and up	A
15 and 16	B	14 and 15	B
13 and 14	C	12 and 13	C
11 and 12	D	10 and 11	D
9 and 10	E		

It has been pointed out above that factors other than age markedly influence performance in individual cases. Sometimes overprotection, overweight, lack of exercise and lack of practice, etc., influence performance more than does a span of one, two or three years of age. Because there are so many variables, classifying by one rather than two years does not add much accuracy. Physical educators of the blind feel that the two-year classification plan is simple and practical but has limitations as does any other usable system.

DESCRIPTIONS AND PROCEDURES OF TESTING
Basketball Throw for Distance
(Boys and Girls)

Use a 7-ft circle, raised, if possible. A device similar to a shot put ring in front may be used. Any style of throw may be permitted, but the contestant must stay in the ring. Measure from the front part of the ring to where the ball first strikes the ground. Three trials are permitted.

Football Punt for Distance
(Boys)

Mark off the landing area with parallel lines, 5-yds apart. The contestant may not cross the restraining line. The edge of a grass surface serves well as a restraining line. The measurement is made at right angles to the restraining line to the point where the football first strikes the ground. A ball kicked to the right or left will lose ground when the kick is measured correctly. The ball must be dropped from the hands and cannot be kicked from the ground. Three trials are permitted.

Hanging (Girls)

The student should grasp the bar with forward grip (back of hands to the face). Hang so that the feet do not touch the floor or ground. Both hands must be kept on the bar at all times. Do not permit shifting from one hand to the other. You may wish to have three or four girls hang at once, and then note the time each drops to the floor. One trial is permitted.

Pull-Ups (Boys)

The student should grasp the bar with the forward grip (back of hands to the face). He then raises his body by his arms until his chin can be placed over the bar, and then he lowers his body to a full hang as in the starting position. Contestants must not kick. The exercise is repeated as many times as possible. One trial is permitted.

Pull-Ups (Girls)

Adjust a bar so that it will be approximately at the height of the nipple. Use an overhand grasp. The legs are extended under the bar and should be prevented from slipping by a mat or the teacher's foot. The arms should form an angle of 90° with the body line, and the body line should form an angle of 45° with the floor. From this position, the pupil raises her body by her arms until the chest touches the bar, then lowers her body to a full hang. The exercise is repeated. Do not count pull-ups in which the student fails to keep the body straight, come to a full extension of the arms or touch the chest to the bar. No resting is permitted. A contestant is given only one trial.

Rope Climb (Boys)[7]

The rope should be 1 1/2 to 2 1/2 in thick. The height to be climbed is 16 ft. Each contestant is allowed two trials, using any style of climbing. Hands and feet are commonly used. Stop the watch when a boy's hand reaches the 16-ft mark.

Rope Jump (Boys and Girls)

The time limit is two minutes. The contestant may use any style of jumping rope. Every time the student jumps or steps over the rope, it should be counted as one jump. The rope must pass overhead between jumps. For inexperienced students, this may be more of a stepping over activity, rather than a jumping event. One trial is permitted.

Running Fifty Yards (Boys and Girls)

Where possible, the totally blind runner should use guide wires stretched between poles. If guide wires are not available, other less satisfactory methods can be used. First, a sighted student may run in front of the totally blind runner. The student who has vision should shout or blow a whistle. Second, the teacher may blow a whistle at the finish line. Third, a sightless student may run with one who has vision, holding hands. If the sighted student tends to pull his companion, an inaccurate result may be obtained. One trial is permitted.

Running 600 Yards (Boys and Girls)

Totally blind runners should use guide wires, or if necessary,

---

[7]Girls may climb ropes, but no achievement scales are available for them.

run with a partner who has vision. Students with vision should be placed at each end of the guide wire to shout and thus help the sightless runner make better turns. When runners are paired, they should be of comparable ability. One trial is permitted.

Shuttle Run (Boys and Girls)

Some modifications are necessary for this event. Visually handicapped children merely touch the ground instead of picking up blocks. Two lines are established 30-ft apart and the student runs back and forth twice, touching the floor or ground the three times he turns. Sighted students should be stationed 5-ft behind each line and should shout to guide the sightless runner. The teacher should tell the runner when to turn. Use guide wires, if available. Allow two trials.

A shuttle run course may be set up in such a way that sightless children will perform better and more independently. In a gymnasium, a mat surface is helpful. A mat 30-ft long and 5-ft wide is ideal, but a wrestling surface can be used. In a gymnasium, a line may be established 30-ft from a wall which serves as a second or turning line. Outdoors, a wall or cyclone fence may be used for the same purpose. Also outdoors, the edge of a surface can be used for a second or turning line. For example, establish a line 30-ft from the edge of the grass or asphalt surface. By making the identification of one or both lines possible for blind children, improved performance will result. In the great majority of cases, a blind child will enjoy performing more if he requires less assistance.

Sit-Ups, Knee Bent (Boys and Girls)

The student lies on his back on a mat or turf with his knees bent, feet on the floor not more than twelve inches from buttocks. The angle of the knees should be less than 90°. The fingers are clasped behind the head and the elbows are placed squarely on the mat. A partner holds the feet to keep them on the mat at all times. The student brings his head and elbows forward as he *curls* up, touches the knees with elbows, and returns to starting position with his *elbows on the mat* before he starts again. The time limit is one minute. Allow one trial.

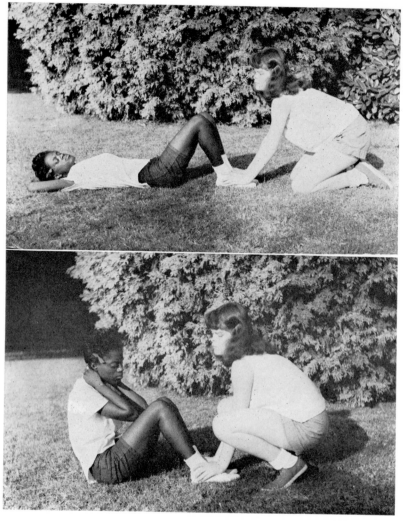

FIGURE 8. Knee bent sit-ups at the California School for the Blind.

Squat-Thrusts (Boys and Girls)

The pupil places his hands on the floor and bends his knees. He thrusts both feet backward until there is a little sag in the back. He jerks his feet forward and stands up. One must stand up at right angles to the floor or ground. Count one for each time the subject correctly completes an action. Only one trial is permitted. The time limit for girls is half a minute and for boys, one minute.

Standing Broad Jump (Boys and Girls)

The contestant stands on the take-off board, swings his arms backward, and bends his knees. The jump is made by extending the knees and swinging forward the arms. Measure from the front edge of the take-off board to the mark made by the heel or other part of the body that touches the ground nearest to the take-off board. Measure to the nearest inch. Both feet must leave the take-off board at the same time, and the contestant must land on both feet. Do not permit a step. The contestant has three trials.

Standing Hop, Step and Jump (Girls)

The girl stands with one foot on the take-off board, hops forward on the same foot, steps forward on the other foot, and leaps forward landing on both feet. From start to finish the performance is continuous without a pause. Measure as in the standing broad jump and to the nearest inch. Allow three trials.

Swimming Twenty Yards (Boys and Girls)

This is a free style swim for speed. If possible, swim without a turn. If a turn must be made in a small pool, deduct one second from the time. Encourage totally blind swimmers to swim alongside of the pool. If possible, also use the lane markers to keep the swimmer in a straight line. Two trials are allowed with not less than fifteen minutes rest.

READING THE SCALES

The scales are read by knowing the classification of the boy or girl and locating the performance in the class column. The score to be given will be found directly opposite either to the right or left. If the exact performance record cannot be found, find the next lowest record listed in the achievement scale and use the score opposite that record. Here are some examples. Class B blind girl runs 50 yd in 10.2 seconds. Her score is 40 points. Class D partially seeing boy broad jumps 6 ft 11 in and gets 95 points.

BASKETBALL THROW FOR DISTANCE (GIRLS)
(DISTANCE IN FEET)

| Score | Partially Seeeing Girls | | | | Score | Totally Blind Girls | | | | Score |
	A	B	C	D		A	B	C	D	
5	9	9	7	4	5	8	8	4	2	5
10	12	12	11	7	10	10	10	6	4	10
15	16	16	14	9	15	12	12	8	5	15
20	19	19	17	11	20	14	14	10	6	20
25	23	23	20	13	25	16	16	12	7	25
30	26	26	23	15	30	18	18	14	8	30
35	30	30	26	18	35	20	20	16	10	35
40	33	33	29	20	40	22	22	18	11	40
45	37	37	32	22	45	24	24	20	12	45
50	40	40	35	24	50	26	26	22	13	50
55	43	43	38	26	55	28	28	24	14	55
60	46	46	41	28	60	30	30	26	16	60
65	49	49	44	30	65	32	32	28	17	65
70	52	52	46	32	70	34	34	30	19	70
75	55	55	49	34	75	36	36	32	20	75
80	58	58	52	36	80	38	38	34	22	80
85	61	61	54	38	85	40	40	36	23	85
90	64	64	57	40	90	42	42	38	25	90
95	67	67	60	42	95	44	44	40	26	95
100	70	70	63	46	100	46	46	42	28	100

HANGING (GIRLS)
(TIME IN SECONDS)

Score	A	B	C & D
5	4	5	4
10	8	10	8
15	12	15	12
20	16	20	16
25	20	25	20
30	24	30	24
35	28	35	28
40	32	40	32
45	36	45	36
50	40	50	40
55	47	57	50
60	55	65	60
65	67	77	70
70	80	90	80
75	92	102	90
80	105	115	100
85	117	127	110
90	130	140	120
95	142	152	132
100	160	170	150

GIRLS' STANDING BROAD JUMP
(DISTANCE IN FEET AND INCHES)

Score	A	B	C	D	Score
5	2-3	2-1	1-8	1-0	5
10	2-9	2-7	2-2	1-6	10
15	3-0	2-10	2-6	1-10	15
20	3-3	3-1	2-10	2-1	20
25	3-6	3-4	3-1	2-5	25
30	3-9	3-7	3-4	2-8	30
35	4-0	3-10	3-7	3-0	35
40	4-3	4-1	3-10	3-3	40
45	4-6	4-4	4-1	3-7	45
50	4-9	4-7	4-4	3-10	50
55	5-0	4-10	4-6	4-0	55
60	5-2	5-0	4-8	4-2	60
65	5-4	5-2	4-10	4-4	65
70	5-6	5-4	5-0	4-6	70
75	5-8	5-6	5-2	4-8	75
80	5-10	5-8	5-4	4-10	80
85	6-0	5-10	5-6	5-0	85
90	6-2	6-0	5-8	5-2	90
95	6-6	6-4	6-0	5-6	95
100	7-0	6-9	6-6	6-0	100

STANDING HOP, STEP AND JUMP (GIRLS)
(DISTANCE IN FEET AND INCHES)

Score	A & B	C	D	Score
5	7-4	6-0	4-6	5
10	8-8	7-2	5-10	10
15	9-5	8-2	6-10	15
20	10-0	9-0	7-7	20
25	10-7	9-7	8-2	25
30	11-2	10-2	8-9	30
35	11-9	10-9	9-4	35
40	12-4	11-4	9-11	40
45	12-11	11-11	10-6	45
50	13-6	12-6	11-0	50
55	14-2	13-1	11-5	55
60	15-0	13-8	11-10	60
65	15-8	14-3	12-3	65
70	16-4	14-10	12-8	70
75	17-0	15-5	13-1	75
80	17-8	16-0	13-6	80
85	18-4	16-7	14-0	85
90	19-0	17-2	14-6	90
95	19-10	18-0	15-0	95
100	21-0	19-0	16-0	100

MODIFIED PUSH-UPS (GIRLS)

Score	A & B	C & D
5	1	1
10	3	3
15	5	5
20	7	7
25	9	9
30	10	11
35	11	12
40	12	14
45	13	15
50	14	17
55	16	19
60	18	21
65	21	23
70	24	26
75	28	30
80	32	34
85	37	39
90	43	45
95	50	52
100	60	60

FIFTY-YARD DASH (TIME IN SECONDS AND TENTHS)

Partially Seeing Girls Score	A	B	C	D	Totally Blind Girls Score	A	B	C	D	Score
5	15.0	14.7	16.1	18.2	5	17.3	17.5	19.0	22.2	5
10	14.4	14.0	15.4	17.4	10	16.5	16.6	18.2	21.2	10
15	13.8	13.4	14.7	16.6	15	15.7	15.8	17.4	20.2	15
20	13.2	12.7	14.0	15.8	20	14.9	15.0	16.7	19.2	20
25	12.6	12.0	13.4	15.0	25	14.1	14.3	16.0	18.2	25
30	12.0	11.5	12.7	14.2	30	13.4	13.6	15.2	17.2	30
35	11.5	11.0	12.1	13.4	35	12.8	12.9	14.4	16.2	35
40	11.0	10.5	11.5	12.6	40	12.2	12.3	13.6	15.2	40
45	10.5	10.0	10.9	11.8	45	11.6	11.7	12.8	14.2	45
50	10.0	9.6	10.3	11.0	50	11.0	11.2	12.0	13.3	50
55	9.8	9.4	10.0	10.6	55	10.6	10.8	11.6	12.9	55
60	9.6	9.2	9.8	10.3	60	10.3	10.4	11.2	12.4	60
65	9.3	9.0	9.5	9.9	65	10.0	10.1	10.8	12.0	65
70	9.1	8.8	9.2	9.6	70	9.7	9.8	10.4	11.5	70
75	8.8	8.5	8.9	9.2	75	9.4	9.5	10.0	11.1	75
80	8.5	8.2	8.6	9.0	80	9.0	9.1	9.6	10.5	80
85	8.2	7.9	8.4	8.8	85	8.6	8.7	9.2	10.0	85
90	7.9	7.6	8.1	8.5	90	8.2	8.3	8.8	9.5	90
95	7.5	7.2	7.5	8.2	95	7.8	7.9	8.4	9.0	95
100	6.5	6.2	6.7	7.3	100	7.3	7.4	7.8	8.4	100

600-YARD RUN-WALK (TIME IN MINUTES AND SECONDS)

Partially	Seeing	Girls			Totally	Blind	Girls			
Score	A	B	C	D	Score	A	B	C	D	Score
5	5:10	5:08	5:16	5:38	5	6:15	6:15	6:27	7:50	5
10	4:58	4:56	5:03	5:25	10	6:00	6:00	6:10	7:25	10
15	4:47	4:45	4:52	5:13	15	5:45	5:45	5:54	7:00	15
20	4:36	4:34	4:41	5:00	20	5:30	5:30	5:37	6:35	20
25	4:25	4:23	4:30	4:47	25	5:15	5:15	5:21	6:10	25
30	4:14	4:12	4:19	4:34	30	5:00	5:00	5:06	5:55	30
35	4:03	4:01	4:08	4:21	35	4:45	4:45	4:50	5:30	35
40	3:52	3:50	3:57	4:08	40	4:30	4:30	4:35	5:05	40
45	3:41	3:39	3:46	3:56	45	4:15	4:15	4:19	4:40	45
50	3:30	3:28	3:35	3:45	50	4:00	4:00	4:03	4:15	50
55	3:24	3:21	3:29	3:39	55	3:53	3:53	3:56	4:05	55
60	3:17	3:14	3:22	3:32	60	3:46	3:46	3:49	3:58	60
65	3:11	3:08	3:15	3:25	65	3:39	3:39	3:42	3:51	65
70	3:04	3:01	3:08	3:19	70	3:32	3:32	3:35	3:44	70
75	2:58	2:55	3:02	3:13	75	3:25	3:25	3:28	3:37	75
80	2:51	2:48	2:55	3:07	80	3:18	3:18	3:21	3:31	80
85	2:44	2:41	2:48	3:00	85	3:11	3:11	3:14	3:25	85
90	2:37	2:34	2:41	2:52	90	3:04	3:04	3:07	3:20	90
95	2:30	2:27	2:34	2:45	95	2:57	2:57	3:00	3:15	95
100	2:10	2:09	2:18	2:30	100	2:25	2:25	2:30	2:50	100

MODIFIED PULL-UPS (GIRLS)
(NUMBER OF PULL-UPS SAME FOR ALL CLASSES)

Score	Pull-ups
5	2
10	4
15	6
20	8
25	10
30	11
35	13
40	15
45	18
50	20
55	22
60	24
65	26
70	28
75	30
80	32
85	34
90	36
95	38
100	40

TWO-MINUTE ROPE JUMP (GIRLS (NUMBER OF JUMPS)

Score	A	B	C	D	Score
5	10	10	5	5	5
10	20	20	10	10	10
15	30	30	15	15	15
20	40	40	20	20	20
25	50	50	30	25	25
30	60	60	40	30	30
35	70	70	50	35	35
40	80	80	60	40	40
45	90	90	70	45	45
50	100	100	80	50	50
55	115	115	93	57	55
60	130	130	105	64	60
65	145	145	118	71	65
70	160	160	130	78	70
75	175	175	143	85	75
80	190	190	155	92	80
85	205	205	168	99	85
90	220	220	180	106	90
95	235	235	193	113	95
100	250	250	205	120	100

ONE-MINUTE KNEE BENT SIT-UPS (GIRLS) (SAME FOR ALL CLASSES)

Score	Sit-ups
5	8
10	11
15	14
20	16
25	18
30	20
35	21
40	23
45	24
50	25
55	27
60	28
65	30
70	31
75	33
80	34
85	36
90	38
95	41
100	48

THIRTY-SECOND SQUAT-THRUSTS (GIRLS) (NUMBER OF SQUAT-THRUSTS)

Score	A	B	C	D	Score
5	4	2			5
10	5	3	1		10
15	6	4	2		15
20	7	5	3	1	20
25	8	6	4	2	25
30	9	7	5	3	30
35	10	8	6	4	35
40	11	9	7	5	40
45	12	10	8	6	45
50	13	11	9	7	50
55	14	12	10	8	55
60	15	13	11	9	60
65	16	14	12	10	65
70	17	15	13	11	70
75	18	16	14	12	75
80	19	17	15	13	80
85	20	18	16	14	85
90	21	19	17	15	90
95	22	20	18	16	95
100	23	21	19	17	100

SHUTTLE RUN—GIRLS (TIME IN SECONDS AND TENTHS)

Partially Seeing Girls Score	A	B	C	D	Totally Blind Girls Score	A	B	C	D	Score
5	15.1	15.3	15.5	15.9	5	19.4	19.2	19.6	20.5	5
10	14.5	14.7	14.9	15.3	10	18.8	18.6	19.0	19.9	10
15	14.1	14.3	14.6	15.0	15	18.3	18.1	18.5	19.5	15
20	13.7	13.9	14.3	14.7	20	17.8	17.6	18.0	19.1	20
25	13.5	13.7	14.1	14.5	25	17.3	17.1	17.5	18.8	25
30	13.3	13.5	13.9	14.3	30	16.8	16.6	17.0	18.5	30
35	13.1	13.3	13.7	14.1	35	16.3	16.1	16.5	18.2	35
40	12.9	13.1	13.5	13.9	40	15.8	15.6	16.0	17.9	40
45	12.7	12.9	13.3	13.7	45	15.5	15.3	15.7	17.6	45
50	12.5	12.7	13.1	13.5	50	15.2	15.0	15.4	17.3	50
55	12.2	12.4	12.8	13.2	55	14.9	14.7	15.1	17.0	55
60	12.0	12.2	12.6	13.0	60	14.6	14.4	14.8	16.7	60
65	11.8	12.0	12.4	12.8	65	14.3	14.1	14.5	16.4	65
70	11.6	11.8	12.2	12.6	70	14.0	13.8	14.2	16.1	70
75	11.4	11.6	12.0	12.4	75	13.7	13.5	13.9	15.7	75
80	11.2	11.4	11.8	12.2	80	13.4	13.2	13.6	15.2	80
85	11.0	11.2	11.6	12.0	85	13.1	12.9	13.3	14.8	85
90	10.8	11.0	11.4	11.8	90	12.8	12.6	13.0	14.0	90
95	10.5	10.7	11.1	11.5	95	12.4	12.2	12.6	13.2	95
100	9.5	9.7	10.1	10.5	100	10.8	10.6	11.0	11.5	100

TWENTY-YARD FREE STYLE SWIM (GIRLS)
(TIME IN SECONDS)

Partially Score	Seeing A	Girls B	C	D	Totally Score	Blind A	Girls B	C	D	Score
5	48	48	57	65	5	57	57	67	85	5
10	44	44	52	60	10	52	52	62	79	10
15	40	40	47	55	15	47	47	57	73	15
20	38	38	45	53	20	45	45	54	69	20
25	36	36	42	50	25	42	42	51	65	25
30	34	34	40	48	30	40	40	48	61	30
35	32	32	37	45	35	37	37	45	57	35
40	30	30	35	43	40	35	35	42	53	40
45	28	28	32	40	45	32	32	39	49	45
50	26	26	30	38	50	30	30	36	45	50
55	25	25	29	37	55	28	28	34	43	55
60	24	24	28	36	60	27	27	33	42	60
65	23	23	27	35	65	26	26	32	40	65
70	22	22	26	34	70	25	25	31	38	70
75	21	21	25	33	75	24	24	30	36	75
80	19	19	23	31	80	23	23	28	35	80
85	18	18	22	30	85	22	22	27	33	85
90	17	17	21	29	90	21	21	26	31	90
95	16	16	20	28	95	19	19	24	29	95
100	14	14	18	25	100	16	16	20	25	100

BASKETBALL THROW FOR PARTIALLY SEEING BOYS
(DISTANCE IN FEET)

Score	A	B	C	D	E	Score
5	20	15	11	7	3	5
10	25	20	15	11	7	10
15	30	25	19	14	9	15
20	35	30	23	17	11	20
25	40	35	27	20	13	25
30	45	40	31	23	15	30
35	50	45	35	26	17	35
40	55	49	39	29	19	40
45	60	53	43	32	21	45
50	65	57	47	35	23	50
55	70	61	50	37	25	55
60	75	65	54	39	27	60
65	80	69	57	41	28	65
70	85	73	61	43	30	70
75	90	77	64	45	31	75
80	95	81	67	47	33	80
85	100	85	70	50	35	85
90	105	90	75	55	38	90
95	110	95	80	60	43	95
100	120	105	90	70	48	100

BASKETBALL THROW FOR TOTALLY BLIND BOYS

Score	A	B	C	D	E	Score
5	5	5	4	3	2	5
10	10	10	8	6	4	10
15	15	15	12	9	6	15
20	20	20	16	12	7	20
25	25	25	20	15	9	25
30	30	30	23	17	10	30
35	35	33	26	19	11	35
40	40	37	29	21	13	40
45	45	41	32	23	14	45
50	50	45	35	25	15	50
55	54	49	38	26	17	55
60	58	52	41	27	18	60
65	62	56	44	29	19	65
70	66	59	47	30	20	70
75	70	63	50	32	22	75
80	74	66	53	33	23	80
85	78	70	56	36	24	85
90	85	73	60	40	25	90
95	92	80	65	46	30	95
100	100	87	70	52	35	100

Boy's Football Punt (Distance in yards*)

Score	A		B		C		D		E		Score
5	4	8	2	8	1	5	1	2			5
10	6	10	3	10	3	7	2	4		1	10
15	8	12	4	11	5	8	3	6	1	2	15
20	9	14	5	13	6	9	4	7		3	20
25	11	16	6	14	7	10	5	8	2	4	25
30	13	18	8	16	8	12		9	3	5	30
35	15	20	10	17	9	13	6	10		6	35
40	16	22	12	19	10	14	7	11	4	7	40
45	18	24	13	20	11	15		12		8	45
50	20	26	15	22	12	17	8	13	5	9	50
55	22	28	17	24	14	19	9	14	6	10	55
60	24	30	19	26	16	21	10	15	7	11	60
65	26	32	21	28	18	23	11	16	8	12	65
70	28	34	23	30	20	26	12	17	9	14	70
75	30	36	25	32	22	28	13	18	10	15	75
80	32	39	27	34	23	30	14	20	11	16	80
85	34	42	29	36	25	32	16	22	12	17	85
90	36	46	31	38	27	34	19	25	13	18	90
95	40	50	35	42	30	37	22	27	14	19	95
100	44	54	39	47	34	40	25	31	15	21	100

*Distance for partially seeing boys listed on right of each class column. Distance for totally blind listed on the left.

BOYS' ROPE JUMP (TWO MINUTES) (NUMBER OF JUMPS)

Score	A	B	C	D	E	Score
5	13	11	9	7	4	5
10	32	28	23	19	14	10
15	51	46	38	31	23	15
20	70	63	53	43	33	20
25	88	79	66	54	42	25
30	105	95	80	65	50	30
35	122	112	94	77	59	35
40	140	128	107	88	67	40
45	157	144	121	99	76	45
50	175	160	135	110	84	50
55	192	176	149	122	93	55
60	210	193	162	133	101	60
65	227	209	176	144	110	65
70	245	225	190	155	118	70
75	262	242	203	166	127	75
80	280	258	217	177	136	80
85	297	274	231	188	145	85
90	315	290	245	198	153	90
95	332	305	258	209	162	95
100	350	320	270	220	170	100

BOYS' ROPE CLIMB (TIME IN SECONDS)

Score	A	B	C	D	E	Score
5	16.0	19.3	24.5	30.3	40.0	5
10	15.0	18.1	23.0	28.6	37.8	10
15	14.0	16.9	21.5	26.9	35.7	15
20	13.0	15.7	20.0	25.2	33.6	20
25	12.0	14.5	18.5	23.5	31.5	25
30	11.0	13.3	17.0	21.8	29.4	30
35	10.0	12.1	15.5	20.1	27.3	35
40	9.0	10.9	14.0	18.4	25.2	40
45	8.0	9.7	12.5	16.7	23.1	45
50	7.0	8.5	11.0	15.0	21.0	50
55	6.6	8.0	10.5	14.3	19.9	55
60	6.2	7.6	9.9	13.6	18.8	60
65	5.8	7.1	9.4	12.9	17.7	65
70	5.4	6.7	8.8	12.2	16.6	70
75	5.0	6.2	8.3	11.5	15.5	75
80	4.5	5.8	7.7	10.7	14.4	80
85	4.1	5.3	7.2	10.0	13.3	85
90	3.7	4.9	6.6	9.3	12.2	90
95	3.3	4.4	6.1	8.6	11.1	95
100	2.8	4.0	5.5	7.8	10.0	100

	FIFTY-YARD DASH PARTIALLY SEEING BOYS (TIME IN SECONDS AND TENTHS)						FIFTY-YARD DASH FOR BLIND BOYS (TIME IN SECONDS AND TENTHS)					
Score	*A*	*B*	*C*	*D*	*E*	*Score*	*Score*	*A*	*B*	*C*	*D*	*E*	*Score*
5	9.6	10.1	10.7	11.4	12.2	5	5	10.6	11.1	11.8	12.7	13.8	5
10	9.3	9.8	10.4	11.1	11.9	10	10	10.3	10.8	11.5	12.4	13.5	10
15	8.9	9.4	10.0	10.7	11.5	15	15	9.9	10.4	11.1	12.0	13.1	15
20	8.6	9.1	9.7	10.4	11.2	20	20	9.6	10.1	10.8	11.7	12.8	20
25	8.3	8.8	9.4	10.1	10.9	25	25	9.3	9.8	10.5	11.4	12.5	25
30	8.0	8.5	9.1	9.8	10.6	30	30	9.0	9.5	10.2	11.1	12.2	30
35	7.8	8.3	8.9	9.6	10.4	35	35	8.8	9.3	10.0	10.9	12.0	35
40	7.5	8.0	8.6	9.3	10.1	40	40	8.5	9.0	9.7	10.6	11.7	40
45	7.3	7.8	8.4	9.1	9.9	45	45	8.3	8.8	9.5	10.4	11.5	45
50	7.0	7.5	8.1	8.8	9.6	50	50	8.0	8.5	9.2	10.1	11.2	50
55	6.9	7.4	8.0	8.7	9.5	55	55	7.8	8.3	9.0	9.9	11.0	55
60	6.8	7.3	7.9	8.6	9.4	60	60	7.7	8.2	8.9	9.8	10.9	60
65	6.6	7.1	7.7	8.4	9.2	65	65	7.5	8.0	8.7	9.6	10.7	65
70	6.5	7.0	7.6	8.3	9.1	70	70	7.4	7.9	8.6	9.5	10.6	70
75	6.4	6.9	7.5	8.2	9.0	75	75	7.2	7.7	8.4	9.3	10.4	75
80	6.3	6.8	7.4	8.1	8.9	80	80	7.0	7.5	8.2	9.1	10.2	80
85	6.2	6.7	7.3	8.0	8.8	85	85	6.9	7.4	8.1	9.0	10.1	85
90	6.1	6.6	7.2	7.9	8.7	90	90	6.7	7.2	7.9	8.8	9.9	90
95	5.9	6.4	7.0	7.7	8.5	95	95	6.5	7.0	7.7	8.5	9.5	95
100	5.4	5.9	6.5	7.2	8.0	100	100	6.0	6.5	7.1	8.0	8.9	100

	600-YARD RUN-WALK FOR PARTIALLY SEEING BOYS (TIME IN MINUTES AND SECONDS)						600-YARD RUN-WALK FOR BLIND BOYS (Time in Minutes & Seconds)					
Score	A	B	C	D	E	Score	Score	A	B	C	D	E	Score
5	3:06	3:12	3:30	3:48	4:08	5	5	3:45	3:55	4:18	4:40	5:10	5
10	2:45	2:51	3:09	3:27	3:47	10	10	3:34	3:44	4:06	4:28	4:58	10
15	2:36	2:42	3:00	3:18	3:38	15	15	3:23	3:33	3:54	4:15	4:45	15
20	2:27	2:33	2:51	3:09	3:29	20	20	3:12	3:21	3:42	4:03	4:33	20
25	2:23	2:29	2:47	3:05	3:25	25	25	3:02	3:11	3:31	3:52	4:22	25
30	2.18	2:24	2:42	3:00	3:20	30	30	2:52	3:01	3:20	3:40	4:10	30
35	2:15	2:21	2:39	2:57	3:17	35	35	2:42	2:50	3:09	3:29	3:59	35
40	2:10	2:16	2:34	2:52	3:12	40	40	2:34	2:42	3:00	3:20	3:50	40
45	2:07	2:13	2.31	2:49	3:09	45	45	2:28	2:36	2:52	3:12	3:42	45
50	2:05	2:11	2:29	2:47	3:07	50	50	2:23	2:30	2:46	3:06	3:36	50
55	2:03	2:09	2:27	2:45	3:05	55	55	2:20	2:26	2:42	3:02	3:32	55
60	2:01	2:07	2:25	2:43	3:03	60	60	2:17	2:21	2:38	2:57	3:27	60
65	1:59	2:05	2:23	2:41	3:01	65	65	2:14	2:17	2:34	2:53	3:23	65
70	1:56	2:02	2:20	2:38	2:58	70	70	2:10	2:13	2:30	2:49	3:19	70
75	1:54	2:00	2:18	2:36	2:56	75	75	2:07	2:10	2:26	2:45	3:15	75
80	1:52	1:58	2:16	2:34	2:54	80	80	2:04	2:07	2:22	2:40	3:10	80
85	1:49	1:55	2:13	2:31	2:51	85	85	2:00	2:04	2:18	2:36	3:06	85
90	1:45	1:51	2:09	2:27	2:47	90	90	1:57	2:01	2:15	2:33	3:03	90
95	1:37	1:43	2:01	2:19	2:39	95	95	1:53	1:58	2:12	2:30	3:00	95
100	1:26	1:32	1:50	2:08	2:28	100	100	1:38	1:43	1:58	2:15	2:45	100

BOYS' PULL-UPS
(NUMBER OF PULL-UPS)

Score	A	B	C	D	E
2	1				
10	2	1			
18	3	2	1		
26	4	3	2	1	
34	5	4	3		1
42	6	5	4	2	
50	7	6	5	3	
55	8	7	6	4	2
60	9	8	7		
65	10	9	8	5	3
70	11	10	9	6	
75	12	11	10	7	4
80	13	12	11		
85	14	13	12	8	5
90	16	15	14	9	
95	18	17	16	11	6
100	20	19	18	13	8

ONE-MINUTE KNEE BENT SIT-UPS (BOYS)
(SAME FOR ALL CLASSES)

Score	Sit-ups
5	10
10	15
15	19
20	23
25	27
30	30
35	33
40	35
45	38
50	40
55	43
60	45
65	48
70	50
75	53
80	55
85	58
90	60
95	63
100	70

ONE-MINUTE SQUAT-THRUSTS (BOYS)
(NUMBER OF SQUAT-THRUSTS)

A	B	C	D	E	Score
6	3				4
8	5	2			8
10	7	4	1		12
12	9	6	3		16
14	11	8	5	2	20
16	13	10	7	4	24
18	15	12	9	6	28
20	17	14	11	8	32
22	19	16	13	10	36
24	21	18	15	12	40
26	23	20	17	14	44
28	25	22	19	16	48
30	27	24	21	18	52
31	28	25	22	19	55
32	29	26	23	20	58
33	30	27	24	21	61
34	31	28	25	22	64
35	32	29	26	23	67
36	33	30	27	24	70
37	34	31	28	25	73
38	35	32	29	26	76
39	36	33	30	27	79
40	37	34	31	28	82
41	38	35	32	29	85
42	39	36	33	30	88
43	40	37	34	31	91
44	41	38	35	32	94
45	42	39	36	33	97
46	43	40	37	34	100

SHUTTLE RUN FOR PARTIALLY
SEEING BOYS
(TIME IN SECONDS AND TENTHS)

Score	A	B	C	D	E	Score
5	13.3	13.5	14.0	14.6	15.7	5
10	12.9	13.1	13.6	14.2	15.3	10
15	12.6	12.8	13.3	13.9	15.0	15
20	12.3	12.5	13.0	13.6	14.7	20
25	12.0	12.2	12.7	13.3	14.4	25
30	11.8	12.0	12.5	13.1	14.2	30
35	11.6	11.8	12.3	12.9	14.0	35
40	11.4	11.6	12.1	12.7	13.8	40
45	11.2	11.4	11.9	12.5	13.6	45
50	11.0	11.2	11.7	12.3	13.4	50
55	10.9	11.1	11.6	12.2	13.3	55
60	10.7	10.9	11.4	12.0	13.1	60
65	10.6	10.8	11.3	11.9	13.0	65
70	10.5	10.7	11.2	11.8	12.9	70
75	10.3	10.5	11.0	11.6	12.7	75
80	10.2	10.4	10.9	11.5	12.6	80
85	10.1	10.3	10.8	11.4	12.5	85
90	10.0	10.2	10.7	11.3	12.2	90
95	9.8	10.0	10.5	11.1	12.0	95
100	9.0	9.2	9.6	10.1	11.0	100

SHUTTLE RUN FOR BLIND BOYS
(TIME IN SECONDS AND TENTHS)

Score	A	B	C	D	E	Score
5	15.0	15.3	16.0	17.5	20.5	5
10	14.5	14.8	15.5	17.0	20.0	10
15	14.0	14.3	15.0	16.5	19.6	15
20	13.7	14.0	14.7	16.2	19.1	20
25	13.4	13.7	14.4	15.9	18.8	25
30	13.1	13.4	14.1	15.6	18.4	30
35	12.8	13.1	13.8	15.3	18.1	35
40	12.5	12.8	13.5	15.0	17.8	40
45	12.2	12.5	13.2	14.7	17.4	45
50	12.0	12.3	13.0	14.5	17.2	50
55	11.8	12.1	12.8	14.3	17.0	55
60	11.6	11.9	12.6	14.1	16.7	60
65	11.4	11.7	12.4	13.9	16.5	65
70	11.2	11.5	12.2	13.7	16.2	70
75	11.0	11.3	12.0	13.5	16.0	75
80	10.8	11.1	11.8	13.3	15.8	80
85	10.6	10.9	11.6	13.0	15.4	85
90	10.3	10.6	11.3	12.6	15.0	90
95	10.0	10.3	11.0	12.2	14.2	95
100	9.0	9.3	10.0	11.0	12.5	100

TWENTY-YARD FREE STYLE SWIM
FOR PARTIALLY SEEING BOYS
(TIME IN SECONDS)

Score	A	B	C	D	E	Score
5	30.5	35.2	40.0	46.6	54.2	5
10	29.0	33.4	38.0	44.2	51.5	10
15	27.5	31.6	36.0	41.8	48.6	15
20	26.0	29.8	34.0	39.4	45.8	20
25	24.5	28.0	32.0	37.0	43.0	25
30	23.0	26.2	30.0	34.6	40.2	30
35	21.5	24.4	28.0	32.2	37.4	35
40	20.0	22.6	26.0	29.8	34.6	40
45	18.5	20.8	24.0	27.4	31.8	45
50	17.0	19.0	22.0	25.0	29.0	50
55	16.3	18.2	21.1	24.0	27.9	55
60	15.6	17.4	20.2	23.0	26.8	60
65	14.9	16.6	19.3	22.0	25.7	65
70	14.2	15.8	18.4	21.0	24.6	70
75	13.5	15.0	17.5	20.0	23.5	75
80	12.8	14.2	16.6	19.0	22.4	80
85	12.1	13.4	15.7	18.0	21.3	85
90	11.4	12.6	14.8	17.0	20.2	90
95	10.7	11.8	13.9	16.0	19.1	95
100	10.0	11.0	13.0	15.0	18.0	100

TWENTY-YARD SWIM
FOR TOTALLY BLIND BOYS
(TIME IN SECONDS)

Score	A	B	C	D	E	Score
5	35.2	39.0	44.0	50.5	57.1	5
10	33.4	37.0	41.7	47.8	54.2	10
15	31.6	35.0	39.5	45.2	51.3	15
20	29.8	33.0	37.3	42.6	48.4	20
25	28.0	31.0	35.1	40.0	45.5	25
30	26.2	29.0	32.9	37.4	42.6	30
35	24.4	27.0	30.7	34.8	39.7	35
40	22.6	25.0	28.5	32.2	36.8	40
45	20.8	23.0	26.2	29.6	33.9	45
50	19.0	21.0	24.0	27.0	31.0	50
55	18.2	20.1	23.0	25.9	29.8	55
60	17.4	19.2	22.0	24.8	28.6	60
65	16.6	18.3	21.0	23.7	27.4	65
70	15.8	17.4	20.0	22.6	26.2	70
75	15.0	16.5	19.0	21.5	25.0	75
80	14.2	15.6	18.0	20.4	23.8	80
85	13.4	14.7	17.0	19.3	22.6	85
90	12.6	13.8	16.0	18.2	21.4	90
95	11.8	12.9	15.0	17.1	20.2	95
100	11.0	12.0	14.0	16.0	19.0	100

STANDING BROAD JUMP FOR BOYS
(DISTANCE IN FEET AND INCHES)

Score	A	B	C	D	E	Score
5	4-3	3-9	3-3	2-3	1-9	5
10	4-9	4-3	3-9	2-9	2-3	10
15	5-3	4-9	4-3	3-3	2-6	15
20	5-6	5-0	4-6	3-6	2-10	20
25	5-9	5-3	4-9	3-9	3-1	25
30	6-0	5-6	5-0	4-0	3-4	30
35	6-3	5-9	5-3	4-3	3-7	35
40	6-6	6-0	5-6	4-6	3-10	40
45	6-9	6-3	5-8	4-9	4-0	45
50	7-0	6-5	5-10	5-0	4-2	50
55	7-2	6-7	6-0	5-2	4-4	55
60	7-4	6-9	6-2	5-4	4-6	60
65	7-6	6-11	6-4	5-6	4-8	65
70	7-8	7-1	6-6	5-8	4-10	70
75	7-10	7-3	6-8	5-10	5-0	75
80	8-0	7-5	6-10	6-0	5-2	80
85	8-2	7-7	7-0	6-2	5-4	85
90	8-4	7-10	7-3	6-4	5-6	90
95	8-8	8-3	7-8	6-8	5-9	95
100	9-2	8-9	8-2	7-2	6-2	100

Chapter 13

A GUIDE FOR PHYSICAL EDUCATION
TEACHERS OF THE BLIND

Hundreds of times the writer has been asked by people all over the world for information on physical education for blind children. Most of these queries come from students and teachers who have little or no knowledge of the subject. But there are also teachers and administrators seeking up-to-date information so that they can construct a good curriculum in physical education for their blind pupils. In this chapter such a curriculum is suggested.

Because the objectives of physical education for blind children are similar to those for programs for seeing boys and girls, it does not necessarily follow that the ideal curriculum is the same. It is rather evident that there are some activities, such as baseball and basketball, carried on in the public schools from which seeing boys and girls will benefit much more than their sightless peers. Since some of these activities are very popular, it cannot be expected that they will be dropped in favor of others in which blind children can more actively participate. However, teachers in public schools could introduce some activities suitable for blind students which would not weaken or alter the aims of the program for seeing boys and girls. Thus, blind children would gain tremendously, and their seeing peers would lose nothing. It is unlikely that public schools would adopt the curriculum presented here as a whole, but teachers may use parts of it to advantage. In any event, the guide indicates a curriculum which results in as much development in blind children as is evident in physical education programs for seeing children in public schools. This is the belief of a great majority of physical educators in residential schools for the blind.

Usually, residential schools for the blind do not follow the curriculum in physical education constructed by public schools for their seeing pupils, nor do they spend the same percentages of time on similar activities. Two of the reasons for this are: (a) the value of some physical education activities is not the same for blind as for seeing children (of course, schools for the blind might be expected to select those activities which would be of most benefit to their students); and (b) most residential schools have some facilities not available in all public schools, particularly on the elementary level. A swimming pool is one such facility.

Another way in which residential schools for the blind usually differ from public schools is that they have men and women physical educators to conduct the program on the elementary as well as the secondary level. A common practice in public schools is to assign a classroom teacher to this duty. Thus, public schools find it more difficult to divide the sexes as early as has been found satisfactory for blind children in residential schools. The fact that some blind children are old for their grade level contributes toward the desirability of early separation of sexes. This separation should not be complete.

It is desirable to plan some coeducational activities during the physical education class period. At least one period out of every ten can well be devoted to such activities. Folk, square and social dancing come first to mind, but swimming, skating, hiking, bowling, relays, shuffleboard, giant volleyball and modified softball should not be overlooked.

After teaching physical education to blind children for twenty-five years, the writer has developed some firm beliefs of what constitutes a good program for visually handicapped children. The guide presented here is merely a suggestion. Conditions existing in a school will determine which activities can be used to best advantage. However, it is important to offer an all-around physical education program rather than feature only a limited number of activities and neglect others.

The games, contests, relays and races listed in the guide below can be found elsewhere in this book. The index should be consulted for page numbers. Since rhythms and tumbling stunts require little or no adaptation, detailed descriptions of these activities were not included. However, suitable activities in this area have been described in detail by Van Hagen, Dexter and Williams in *Physical*

Education in the Elementary School.[1] The page numbers listed after rhythms, dances, apparatus activities and stunts refer to page numbers in this comprehensive book. Of course, the teacher will need up-to-date books on gymnastics, swimming, bowling, wrestling, track and field, etc.

Certainly, activities should vary somewhat from teacher to teacher and year to year. Here is the writer's suggested guide which may be used as a basis for a good, all-around physical education program for visually handicapped boys and girls.

The American Association of Health, Physical Education and Recreation recommends thirty minutes each day for organized physical education for Grades 1, 2, 3 and 4. The recommendation is that one hour daily should be allotted to organized physical education, including dressing, for intermediate, junior high and senior high school students. These recommendations have been adopted by the Physical Education Workshop of the American Association of Instructors of the Blind.[2]

PRIMARY

It is recommended that thirty minutes each day be allotted to physical education on this level as follows.

25%	Running games
20%	Swimming
20%	Rhythms or dance
10%	Calisthenics
10%	Apparatus
10%	Hiking or walking
5%	Stunts

Games

Animal blind man's buff	Hide and seek
Animal chase	Midnight
Bear, wolf and sheep	Mousetrap
Boiler, boiler, boiler, blue	The ocean is stormy

1. VAN HAGEN, W., DEXTER, G., and WILLIAMS, J.: *Physical Education in the Elementary School.* California State Department of Education, Sacramento, California, 1951, 1008 p.p.

2. *Proceedings of American Association of Instructors of the Blind,* 1954. P. 76.

Games (Continued)

Boiler burst

Call ball

Flowers and the wind

Flying Dutchman

Follow the leader

Partner tag

Sardines

Slap tag

Stalking

Tommy Tiddler's ground

Swimming

The Red Cross Swimming Program should be begun.

Rhythms and Dance

Bean Porridge Hot, p. 433

Carrousel, p. 436

Children's Polka, p. 437

Dance of Greeting, p. 377

London Bridge, p. 380

Marusaki, p. 381

Nuts in May, p. 382

Sleeping Man, p. 387

Snail, p. 387

Thread Follows the Needle, p. 454

Two-step, p. 454

Apparatus and Stunts

Besides hanging and traveling on the horizontal ladder, students should swing on a climbing rope. A child grasps the rope, picks up his feet, and swings as long as he can. His feet and legs are not to be used to support the weight of the body.

Also, simple tumbling stunts should be taught, including somersaults, forward roll, kneel down and jump to feet, frog stand, armless sit down and rise and deep squat. Another stunt is to bend forward, touch the floor with the palms of the hand, keeping the knees stiff.

Apparatus

Fence climbing, p. 393

Hang and drop, p. 393

Ladder walking, p. 393

Money swing, p. 393

Pole and rope climbing, p. 460

Stair climbing, p. 461

Stunts

Airplane zooming, p. 393

Climb through stick, p. 393

Human rocker, p. 459

Measuring worm, p. 460

Seal walk, p. 461

Orientation

For suggestions on activities which will develop orientation skills, it would be well to read pages 103 through 106 of this book. Some games particularly good for the purpose are blind man's buff, belled cat and bell tag. The teacher should emphasize independent travel to and from the physical education class. To get a spatial conception of the gymnasium or play room, the child should be encouraged to explore independently. Hiking or walking, especially when cues are identified, is very valuable. To overcome fear, the teacher should encourage rapid running and jumping from low heights.

INTERMEDIATE GIRLS
(Grades 4, 5 and 6)

It is recommended that forty-five minutes each day be allotted to physical education on this level as follows.

20% Apparatus, calisthenics, stunts
20% Swimming
20% Rhythms and dance (part coeducational)
15% Running games, relays and contests
15% Team games, track and field
10% Hiking

Games

Ball tag	Last couple out
Barley break	Link tag
Birds and snake	Novelty progress
Circle ball	Rattle snake
Crows and cranes	Simon says
Kick baseball	Spud

Swimming

The Red Cross Program is continued.

Races

Cat-tail chase	Quartet race
Centipede overtake	Sack race
Chariot race	Three-legged race
Chinaman's race	Trio race
Crawling race	Wheelbarrow race

Relays

Backward all fours relay

Bicycle tire relay

Caterpillar relay

Centipede Relay

Couple relay

Dressing relay

Lame dog relay

Military relay

Pass through hoop relay

Rope skip relay

Sack relay

Siamese twins relay

Tandem relay

Three-legged relay

Contests

Low bridge elimination

Numbers

Push ball

Rope jumping

Stunt elimination

Tug-of-war

Weather vane

Rhythms and Dance

Bleking, p. 502

Crested Hen, p. 600

Fun on the Green, p. 697

Heel and Toe Polka, p. 607

Minuet, p. 608

Our Little Girl, p. 512

Seven Jumps, p. 517

Shoemaker's Dance, p. 520

Three-step, p. 707

Turn Around Me, p. 617

Stunts

Back spring, p. 715

Backward roll, p. 527

Camel walk, p. 715

Crab run, p. 625

Double roll, p. 626

Dive, p. 528

Elephant walk, p. 715

Forearm balance, p. 626

Head and hand stand, p. 850

Hand push, p. 627

Heel knock, p. 627

Human ball, p. 627

Jump foot, p. 627

Jumping jack, p. 628

Jump the stick, p. 628

Jump through hands, p. 529

Neck spring, p. 628

Siamese twins, p. 529

Skin the cat, p. 530

Twirling top, p. 629

Twister, p. 718

Orientation

The games of snatch the bacon, winds and other activities develop orientation skills. (For other activities see page 103 through 106 of this book.)

INTERMEDIATE BOYS
(Grades 4, 5 and 6)

It is recommended that forty-five minutes each day be allotted to physical education on this level as follows.

25% Team games, track and field
20% Swimming
20% Apparatus, calisthenics, stunts
15% Running games, contests, and relays
10% Rhythms and dance (coeducational)
10% Hiking

Games

The games listed for intermediate girls are also played by the boys. In addition, the boys play the following games.

Baseball	Hit pin baseball
Bull in the ring	Horses and riders
Chain tag	Japanese torpedo
Football (older boys)	Line blind swat
Forcing the city gates	Round-up
Goal ball	Run, sheep, run

Swimming

The Red Cross Swimming Program should be continued. In addition, some emphasis should be placed on distance swimming.

Contests

Individual combative contests are very popular with boys. Many of them are suitable for sightless boys. Wrestling might be started at this level with some of the older boys. Some instruction in the sport can be given, and short bouts held. This could be a very satisfactory outlet for educationally handicapped boys.

The following combatives are recommended.

Catch and pull tug-of-war	King of the mat
Elbow tug-of-war	Poison snake
Four-way tug	Track and field

Relays and Races

The same relays and races may be used as for intermediate girls. (See page 171.)

Apparatus, Calisthenics and Stunts

The same apparatus activities, calisthenics and stunts may be used as for intermediate girls. (See page 172.)

Orientation

At this level, court ball should be introduced. Hiking can contribute to the student's orientation skills. (See pages 103-106.)

JUNIOR HIGH SCHOOL GIRLS
(Grades 7, 8 and 9)

It is recommended that one hour each day be allotted to physical education on this level as follows.

25% Apparatus, calisthenics, stunts
20% Team games, track and field
15% Rhythms and dance
20% Swimming
10% Relays, contests
10% Coeducational activities (shuffleboard, bowling, hiking, dancing, etc.)

Games

Baseball
Basketball (free throw)
Bowling
Giant volleyball

Goal ball
Kick baseball
Shuffleboard

Swimming

Advanced work in the Red Cross Swimming Program.

Races and Relays

Many of the races and relays for intermediate girls may be used. (See page 171.) In addition, the following can be used.

Leapfrog relay
Obstacle relay, p. 925
Skin the snake relay, p. 816
Wheelbarrow relay

Contests

The same contests for intermediate girls may be used at this level. (See page 172.)

Rhythms and Dance

Badger Gavotte, p. 929

Buffalo Glide, p. 931

Cotton-eyed Joe, p. 600

Rye Waltz, p. 833

Spinning Waltz,

Tantoli, p. 838

To Tur, p. 943

Valeta Waltz, p. 945

Waltz, p. 840

Stunts

In addition to the stunts for intermediate girls (page 172), the following may be used.

Bicycling, p. 948

Chest stand, p. 949

Knee shoulder stand, p. 949

Mountain climber, p. 950

Rocking chair, p. 950

Orientation

At this level the teacher should continue to emphasize the development of orientation skills. (See pages 103-106 of this book.) Particular attention should be paid to new students who enter school at this grade level.

JUNIOR HIGH SCHOOL BOYS
(Grades 7, 8 and 9)

It is recommended that one hour each day be allotted to physical education at this level as follows.

50% Team games, wrestling, track and field

20% Swimming

15% Apparatus, calisthenics, stunts

10% Coeducational activities (dancing, bowling, hiking, shuffleboard, etc.)

5% Relays and contests

Games

Baseball	Mat scramble
Court ball	Push ball
Do or die	Sport X
Football	Team bull in the ring
Goal ball	Team king of the mat
Hit pin baseball	Team medicine ball wrestle
Hold the fort	Tie the prisoner
Kick back	

Swimming

The activities used on this level are similar to those for the intermediate boys, except that more advanced skills are introduced. Some swim meets might be held with teams from other schools.

Contests, Relays and Races

The more advanced activities for intermediate boys listed on page 173, should be continued on this level. In addition, the following may be used:

Battle of knights
Ball wrestle
Rail riding
Rodeo race

Track and Field

A decathlon should be held using Buell's achievement scales. Ten events suitable for the purpose are sit-ups, pull-ups, squat-thrusts, rope climb, rope jump, standing broad jump, shuttle run, 20-yard swim, 50-yard dash and 600-yard run. Competition in track and field could be held with other schools.

Wrestling

During the winter months wrestling should be stressed. If possible, interscholastic competition should be held. In any event, instruction should be given in the sport and bouts held on an intramural basis.

Stunts

Beginners' exercises on the horizontal bar, parallel bars and side horse should be taught. Tumbling stunts with a difficulty of more than three points (Appendix J) should be introduced.

HIGH SCHOOL GIRLS
(Grades 10, 11 and 12)

It is recommended that one hour each day be allotted to physical education at this level as follows.

20% Individual and dual sports (track and field, bowling, roller skating, etc.)

20% Apparatus, calisthenics, tumbling

20% Swimming

15% Rhythms and dance

10% Team games

10% Coeducational activities (dancing, shuffleboard, Swimming, softball, etc.)

5% Relays and contests

The program for high school girls will be similar to that for junior high school girls. (See pages 174-175.) Of course, more advanced work will be presented in swimming, rhythms and dance, apparatus and tumbling. If no bowling lane is available on the campus, provisions should be made for bowling at a local lane. Basketball free throwing may be made into a team contest. A decathlon, including hanging, basketball throw, modified push-ups, squat-thrusts, sit-ups, standing broad jump, 20-yard swim, shuttle run, 50-yard dash and 600-yard run, is recommended. Buell's achievement scales serve as a fair basis for competition and physical fitness testing. (See Chapter 12.) It is advisable that play days and dance festivals be held with other schools. Intramural and inter-scholastic competition in swimming and track and field are recommended.

HIGH SCHOOL BOYS
(Grades 10, 11 and 12)

It is recommended that one hour each day be allotted to physical education at this level as follows.

50% Team sports, including wrestling and track and field

20% Swimming

20% Apparatus, calisthenics, tumbling

10% Relays and contests

More advanced work in swimming, tumbling and apparatus will be presented. Intramural and interscholastic competition in wrestling, track and field, and swimming should be emphasized. Some provision should be made for bowling at a local establishment if there is no lane available at the school.

A decathlon should be held using Buell's achievement scales. Ten events suitable for the purpose are sit-ups, pull-ups, squat-thrusts, rope climb, rope jump, standing broad jump, shuttle run, 20-yard swim, 50-yard dash and 600-yard run.

CORRECTIVE PHYSICAL EDUCATION AT ALL LEVELS

If possible, small classes for corrective physical education should be organized at least on the junior and senior high school levels. If competent leadership is available, younger children who need corrective exercises should have an opportunity to perform them.

EXTRA CURRICULAR ACTIVITIES

Intramural leagues should be organized in bowling and other sports which interest the students. Interscholastic competition in bowling, wrestling, track and field and swimming should be organized. Opportunities to participate in hiking, camping, boating, skating, dancing, swimming and other sports should be offered on an extracurricular basis. Provision should be made for attending sporting events from time to time.

Chapter 14

WRESTLING IN THE LIFE OF A BLIND BOY

THE MAJOR PROBLEMS FACED by visually handicapped persons are psychological in nature, rather than physical. Blindness does not prevent one from functioning nearly normally. He can learn to do almost everything performed by the general public, with such obvious exceptions as driving an automobile and activities which absolutely require vision. A visually handicapped person's chief problems come from public apathy, a misdirected sense of pity and a lack of knowledge of the capabilities of blind people. These attitudes expressed or intimated by those around a blind person usually affect him very drastically. Frustrations are commonly experienced, and the individual's sense of security and self-confidence are severely shaken. These problems are usually more difficult to alleviate than the physical problems arising from lack of vision.

Since public attitudes cannot be changed rapidly, the visually handicapped individual must adjust or change in order to adapt to the environment. Such adjustment involves many psychological factors. One of the most important is the development of self-confidence or a feeling of equality with his sighted peers. One gains confidence by achieving success, especially in areas where the general public does not expect it.

To build up confidence and self-esteem, one of the best opportunities available to a visually handicapped boy is competition in interscholastic and intercollegiate wrestling. This is a sport in which he competes on practically even terms with boys who have normal vision. It gives a blind person confidence when he wins without concessions being given to him. The writer has had the exhilarating experience of sharing such initial victories with over 200 blind boys. Everyone who has had contact with a blind boy before and after he has wrestled interscholastically realizes that the sport has made possible a new outlook on life.

Each year more and more blind boys are competing against wrestlers who have normal vision. The past season found more than 500 blind boys in intercollegiate and interscholastic competition, mostly in residential schools for the blind.

With this background in mind, the writer has selected two blind boys to serve as examples, showing what wrestling meant to them. These boys are representative of hundreds of others, some of whom have accomplished just as much or even more in life.

PAUL TAPIA HAS VARIED TALENTS

One day in 1943, at the age of eleven, Paul Tapia picked up a cylindrical object and pulled a pin at the end. The resulting blast knocked him unconscious and burned off his clothes. When Paul again became conscious, he realized that he could only see sunlight. Somehow he managed to reach the nearby highway and was transported to a hospital in Santa Fe, New Mexico. Here began a fight between life and death. For over twenty days Paul was unable to comprehend anything or recognize anyone. A series of operations was performed in which skin was grafted to insure complete movement of the left arm. Later, several eye operations were performed. However, one eye was lost, and vision in the other was below one tenth normal.

After much coaxing on his mother's part, Paul was persuaded to attend the New Mexico School for the Visually Handicapped at Alamogordo. It was not long before he became adjusted to life at the school. Paul became very interested in scouting, but had to participate as a Lone Scout for two years until a troop was organized at the school. He moved up through the ranks rapidly and was chosen to represent his troop at the International Scout Jamboree at Valley Forge, Pennsylvania, in 1950. A year later Paul qualified as an Eagle Scout. Later he participated in the Explorer Program and earned the Silver Award. During the summers of 1951, 1952 and 1953, he served as a staff member of the Philmont Scout Ranch. Of scouting Paul says, "The scouting program has done much for me. My attitudes toward all school activities and toward life were developed and established on the basis of scouting ideals." While in school, Paul demonstrated strong leadership and practiced his scouting ideals so that he was seldom a problem in any way.

Paul Tapia is a fairly religious boy. He attends church regularly and teaches Sunday School. On the other hand, he is not fanatical in this way.

Another side of Paul's life was music. With no more than average ability, but with plenty of purposeful determination, he attained a focal place in the school orchestra, and was pacesetter for the tenor section of the senior chorus. His diligence enabled him to appear as a saxophone soloist, both in school and on extramural programs. He was a key member of an extracurricular boys' glee club.

Although only an average student, Paul worked very hard and conscientiously at his studies to compile a creditable academic record. This was possible in spite of the fact that he was practicing wrestling for an hour and a half every afternoon. In addition, he and some of the other boys arose at six o'clock in the morning to do a little exercising on their own.

In 1945 Paul started wrestling in the 103 lb class. Eight years later he graduated, having won sixty-five matches with no losses. In 1949 he won the basketball throw in the National Meet, and in 1952 he placed first in the rope climb and shot put.

During his freshman year at the University of New Mexico, Paul carried on some musical activities, as he was not eligible for athletic competition. As a sophomore, Paul was eager to go out for the wrestling team, but he found none existed. However, with no coaching and only mediocre competition for practice, Paul Tapia took third place in the Skyline Conference in 1954. For his efforts, the University of New Mexico awarded its first wrestling letter. By the next year a team had been formed, and Paul won four matches by falls and lost none. The fact that he had injuries limited his competition for the season. He so impressed his coaches that an athletic scholarship was awarded to him in his final year of competition. He was elected captain of the team and won seven out of eight matches. Paul was never pinned in his entire wrestling career.

Paul Tapia is grateful to Dr. Neal Quimby, a pioneer in wrestling for the blind, for introducing him to wrestling. It has played a very important role in his life. He once expressed himself in this way: "My high school and college wrestling, with its ups and downs, has come to an end. I did not have quite enough to be a collegiate champion, but I learned a lesson—the lesson of life. In life, as in wrestling, you meet your odds and you learn to overcome them. If you are defeated, you bounce right back and do your best to achieve victory the next time. Personality and character traits developed in wrestling are confidence, determination, persistence, discipline, and respect for an opponent's ability—all of which are essential qualities in some degree in each individual's pattern or philosophy of life. No sport excels wrestling as a builder of total physical fitness. This sport serves to develop desirable character traits, a healthy body and a sound mind."

Dr. Neal Quimby had so much confidence in Paul Tapia that he relinquished his coaching duties to him. Since 1957 Paul has been a successful teacher and coach at the New Mexico School for the Visually Handicapped.

BILL SCHMIDT PERSEVERES

When the writer introduced wrestling at the California School for the Blind in 1946, Bill Schmidt, a seventh grade student, was one of the candidates for the team, and not a very promising one for the first two years. In his first match Bill was pinned in a minute and a half. After two years, Bill's record showed three wins and eleven losses. The important thing, however, is that he had encouragement from the coach and other teachers and an ability to persevere. He did not give up, and in the ninth grade Bill won as many matches as he lost. The next year he really blossomed, with twelve victories in fourteen outings, including a novice tournament championship.

When Bill entered Technical High School in Oakland, California, he and two other blind boys gave a wrestling demonstration before the student body. As a result, the school organized a wrestling team. Bill lost only one match in two years and won city championships in 1951 and 1952.

Of his high school experience Bill says, "Wrestling helped me in making many acquaintances. I also believe that through the sport

I gained a degree of poise and self-confidence which benefited me, not only in high school, but in later years as well. I feel that my teammates and school friends accepted me as an equal."

Before continuing Bill's career in wrestling, it might be well to mention that it was only part of his life, though an important part. In academic work he was maintaining a "B" average. Bill has attended church regularly through the years. In two years of scouting he earned First-Class Rank and some merit badges. Bill served a year as a den chief in the Cub Scout program. Here he showed leadership and a love of younger children that was destined to aid him in later life. Entirely separate from his school activities was a series of public tumbling demonstrations performed with his brother and "Strong Man" Jim Payne. In addition to his athletic skills, this sightless boy was a proficient carpenter and mechanic. He could make or fix a great variety of things. Even the family car responded to his skill.

At San Francisco State College Bill compiled a dual meet record of fourteen wins and six losses in three years of intercollegiate wrestling. The high point of his career occurred in March, 1955, when he won a second place medal in the Far Western AAU Tournament in which all the best college and club wrestlers of the region compete. He lost only to that perennial national champion, "Doc" Melvin Northrup, who took up wrestling to keep from becoming a cripple.

In college Bill made an excellent academic record and did his practice teaching in the eighth grade of a public school. He worked with a class of boys and girls with normal vision by organizing committees to aid him in tasks, such as blackboard work, which could not be performed by a sightless teacher. Bill was able to successfully meet this difficult challenge because of his good personality and fine character, both of which had been partly developed through participation in competitive athletics.

Upon graduation from college the Temple City Public Schools employed Bill to teach the eighth grade. This was the first opportunity for a blind college student to become a full-time teacher in the public schools of California. Up to this time blind teachers had not been employed to teach blind children in a resource room, much less sighted children in a regular classroom. He knew that if he succeeded, others would likely be hired, and if he failed, the door might not open again for years. Bill was successful in teaching sighted children. Today about fifty other blind teachers are employed in the public schools of the state, either in resource rooms or in a regular classroom.

Bill married and is carrying on a normal family life. One evening in 1963 Bill Schmidt was doing some work in the house, while his daughter played outdoors. Since he is totally blind, from time to time he would call to her to reassure himself of her presence. After a series of calls, there was one to which there was no reply. Bill sensed what had happened, and he dashed from the house and dove into the swimming pool in the yard. In his trial he was not able to locate his three-year-old daughter. He surfaced, gulped some air and submerged again. This time he was successful in finding the limp body in the deep end of the pool. He revived her with mouth-to-mouth respiration. Fortunately, he had acquired this knowledge and skill while in school.

Bill has been teaching the same grade for ten years now. During the school year he finds himself busy filling out report cards, attending education conferences, taking university courses and carrying on all the other activities normally associated with teaching. Though blind, his routine is not different from that of any other teacher.

The lesson in perseverance which he learned as a wrestler has helped him to succeed in his life work. He gained much of his perseverance and self-confidence through his early wrestling experiences as well as through his other efforts needed to become a teacher. Athletic competition has played an important role in making Bill Schmidt as successful as he is today.

SUMMARY

Participation in wrestling can assist a blind boy to overcome the psychological problems facing him. If he can overcome these problems, he is much more likely to make a satisfactory adjustment to his environment. Fellow pupils and every staff member should encourage blind athletes, because participation in sports, which requires extra effort, will better prepare them in many ways for living in an adult society.

Chapter 15

CHAMPIONS IN SPITE OF BLINDNESS

IT IS NOT WIDELY KNOWN that blind people have become champions in athletics. They may have had to work much harder than their seeing peers to achieve the same rung of success. However, blind athletes have won honors in wrestling, bowling, golf, crew, swimming, gymnastics, ice skating, football, track and field, dancing and hiking.

Most of the information in this chapter was obtained through the *Bulletin for Physical Educators of the Blind* of which the writer has been editor for the last fourteen years. The information here and the personal file of the writer are the most complete sources of information on blind athletes available. Other sources are a few newspaper clippings in the libraries of Perkins School for the Blind and the American Foundation for the Blind. It is likely that many feats of blind athletes have not come to the writer's attention. However, in some fields, such as wrestling and bowling, there is such a wealth of information that only the outstanding athletes could be included here. Unless otherwise indicated, the athletes mentioned here have little or no useful vision. They have participated in many sports despite their lack of vision.

Wrestling

Visually handicapped wrestlers need ask for no favors in the sport. Only the opponent who is more skillful or in better physical condition can defeat a blind wrestler. Opponents fight hard because they do not wish to lose to a blind athlete if they can help it. The theme of this chapter is that many fine athletes have been unable to avoid being defeated by blind opponents.

It should be made clear that the term *wrestling* is used here to refer to the amateur sport and not the professional sideshow which poses under the same name. All dangerous holds are forbidden by the rules. Serious injuries are rare occurrences.

Perhaps the best known blind athlete is Robert Allman who was featured in a *Saturday Evening Post* article some years ago. In 1936, as a freshman at the University of Pennsylvania, Allman encountered some difficulty in obtaining permission to wrestle from the athletic board. His success with the board, and later on the mat, opened the doors of collegiate athletics to many blind men. Allman was defeated only twice as a freshman. In the next three years he won fifteen matches for the University of Pennsylvania, and placed second in the Eastern Intercollegiate Wrestling Meet each year. As a junior, Allman won the Middle Atlantic AAU 118 lb Championship. In 1939 he was elected captain of the Pennsylvania wrestling team, and the newspapers chose him as the most courageous athlete of the year in the United States. There is no secret to this blind man's success. Allman trained faithfully hour after hour to perfect his holds, counters and escapes. The perseverance he developed on the mat served him well for his life's work in becoming a successful attorney and insurance salesman.

Another outstanding wrestler is Jacob Twersky, who was not pinned in eight years of competition in high school and university. In 1942 Twersky won the New York City Metropolitan Championship in the 121 lb class. The following year he was chosen captain of the New York City College wrestling team. Today he is a successful university professor.

After winning forty-eight consecutive bouts at the Overbrook School for the Blind, Fred Barkovitch (128 lb) duplicated Allman's fine record at the University of Pennsylvania. Barkovitch, who has some useful vision, also won the National AAU Title.

At Baltimore in 1943 Fred Tarrant placed third in the National AAU 155 lb class. He was a student of the New York Institute for the Education of the Blind. Anthony Matter (155 lb) from the same school also finished third in the National AAU Meet held in New York City in 1946.

Gene Manfrini lost only six bouts in close to ninety matches, and still missed winning an intercollegiate championship. He competed for the New York Institute, Columbia University, and wrestled in AAU tournaments. Manfrini's coach, Dick Waite, describes his wrestling in the following words: "Gene has been primarily a counter wrestler from the standing position, using the whizzer hold and the switch series to counter leg tackles. He possesses an uncanny sense of balance and appears to be riding much too high for the normal wrestler. He uses the nelson holds for pinning combinations. From the defensive position he works exclusively for reversals, using powerful switches, rolls and step-overs."

Partially seeing men who made fine records in wrestling are Morton Schlein (Ithaca College, New York), Floyd Austin (Michigan State University), Lupe Torres (University of California at Los Angeles) and Joe Lyons (Baltimore YMCA).

In California partially seeing Lynn Brooks won the 147 lb position on a stronger-than-average team. He won eighteen, while losing eight at San Jose State College. He graduated in 1957 and is now teaching in a public school.

Eugene Spurrier, formerly of the Maryland School for the Blind, and a graduate of Towson State Teachers' College, completed his collegiate wrestling career with a twenty-seven to four record. In 1952 he won a Mason-Dixon Conference Championship in the 123 lb class.

Jim Taylor won wrestling letters for four years at Baldwin Wallace College in Ohio. He graduated in 1958.

At South Dakota State College, Ray Melhoff won seventeen and lost nine bouts. Wrestling did a great deal for Ray in the development of self-confidence and physical ability. It pushed him to do better school work. Coach Warren Wilkinson said of Ray: "I have never worked with or coached a finer boy."

Leonard Ogburn, partially sighted, with a record of 18-2 at Auburn University, won the Southeastern Conference Championship twice. In 1959 he entered the National AAU Wrestling Meet, where competition is held both in Greco-Roman and free style wrestling. Although Leonard was unfamiliar with the former style, he eliminated one national champion. He was eliminated on an unfortunate misunderstanding in thinking that his opponent was pinned, when he was not, according to the referee. He was leading ten to one at the time. Among the best wrestlers of the nation,

Leonard Ogburn won seven out of nine bouts. It is very likely his collegiate record would have been even more impressive if it had not been for the unfortunate development of a health condition which curtailed his wrestling at the end of the second year. At present he is teaching and coaching wrestling at the Virginia School for the Blind.

In 1959 Jesus Monreal won the 114-lb AAU Championship held in San Antonio, Texas. He was the outstanding wrestler in the 1959 Tournament of Schools for the Blind in the Southwest.

Wrestling for Findlay College in Ohio, Buell Messer, partially sighted, compiled a four-year record of twenty-seven wins and thirteen losses. His won-lost performance record would have been even better if he had not wrestled a number of times over his weight to balance team effort. Today he is teaching and coaching at the Wisconsin School for the Visually Handicapped.

While at Southern Illinois University Eugene Edwards won forty bouts and lost only seven. He won an IIAC Championship three times and placed second in the Illinois Invitational Tournament. Upon graduation, he began teaching at the Missouri School for the Blind.

In the toughest conference for wrestling, The Big Eight, Dan Faimon placed fourth for the University of Nebraska in 1962. In this difficult competition, he compiled a collegiate record of twenty-three wins and twenty-four losses. Many of his losses came during the first year of competition.

It is interesting to note that when the University of Nebraska met the University of Missouri in a dual wrestling meet in 1962, each team had two blind wrestlers. As it worked out, they did not meet each other on the mat.

Partially sighted Richard McCauley won the New England AAU 125-lb Championship in wrestling in 1963. A graduate of Perkins School for the Blind, he is also an accomplished distance runner.

The record for winning the most wrestling bouts for the University of Missouri is held by a blind athlete. Rich Adams won twenty-seven matches and lost twelve. He also gained the distinction of having the fastest pin in the history of the university. In 1964 he graduated.

In the table below will be found the won-lost records of other outstanding blind collegiate wrestlers.

Name	Year	College	Won and Lost Record
Holt, Andy	1950-54	N. Carolina U.	10-12-0
Balot, Norman	1951-55	N. Y. City College	15-15-0
Bowden, Stewart	1951-55	U. of Virginia	6- 4-0
Lennox, Ted	1951-55	Michigan State U.	12-12-2
Basler, Jim	1955-59	Macalester, Minn.	24-20-1
Clough, Ray	1958-62	Lincoln U., Pa.	13-10-0
Boyer, Burt	1960-62	Appalachian, N. C.	8- 5-1
Harris, Allen	1964-65	Wayne U., Michigan	19- 1-1
Drewicke, R.	1962-65	U. of Minn., Morris	16-10-1
Cox, Don	1962-64	Virginia Tech	9- 4-0
Rogers, Ed	1964-65	Central Michigan U.	14- 2-1

Not all blind boys are permitted to wrestle. A few years ago a blind athlete sustained a moderately severe ankle sprain from wrestling for a university.[1] The medical department forbade him to participate in any further competition after he recovered. Since the man was a good wrestler, the school lost a good athlete, and the blind individual lost much more. The coach mentioned that wrestling was something the blind boy could do well and from which he could derive much satisfaction. He further pointed out that the medical department was unaware of the real meaning of wrestling to that boy and therefore deprived him of something that was very important to him.

The writer has compiled a five-year Honor Roll of Blind High School Wrestlers.[2] Some of the same problems of selecting an All-American Football Team were faced in this undertaking.

First, there is a great variation in the caliber of competition from state to state, from one athletic association of schools for the blind to another and even from year to year, depending upon the number of participants. In some states, such as Texas and Arkansas, no public school competition exists, so the blind boys do not get many opportunities to prove themselves. Some boys have been overlooked because their coaches did not send in their won and lost records. In any event, all of us should be proud of all the boys

---

1. The name of the university is withheld in the interest of good public relations.
2. See Appendix K.

who are on the Honor Roll and the others who were not listed through no fault of theirs.

Perhaps it should be emphasized that the Honor Roll covers only a period of five years, 1961-1965. Because of this, some outstanding performances which occurred just prior to this period are not included. For example, Edward Harrington of the New York State School for the Blind, Batavia, won forty bouts in a row and placed second in the 1959 AAU Wrestling Meet in Buffalo. For the same reason, such Missouri State Champions as Roland Sykes (1958), Daryl Lauer (1958), Albert Duciaome (1958), Paul Ney (1959) and Rich Adams (1960) are not listed. Also, Charles Abel did not win his 1959 Virginia State Championship during this period.

Teams of blind wrestlers have established some outstanding records. In twenty years the New Mexico School for the Visually Handicapped has lost only six dual meets. Under Dr. Neal Quimby the team won fifty-six consecutive dual meets and had an overall record of 69-2. Since Paul Tapia took over the coaching reins seven years ago, New Mexico has lost four meets, but also established a winning streak of forty-six victories in a row. Other winning streaks have been established by Schools for the Blind in California and Virginia at thirty-one and twenty respectively. Overbrook lost no meets between 1933 and 1938 and went un-defeated during the seasons of 1962 and 1963.

The California School for the Blind and the Colorado School for the Blind host annual wrestling tournaments. In the California event 150 to 170 entries from a dozen local high schools participate in a novice wrestling tournament. The Dr. Charles E. Buell Perpetual Trophy is awarded each year to the outstanding wrestler of the tournament. When the coaches first created this trophy in 1964, it was won by Steve Welch, 138 lb, a student of the California School for the Blind.

In 1965 Bob Harris, a Junior at the Ohio School for the Blind, won the 103 lb AAU Championship for his region. Bob was the first blind boy in this region to win such a title. The score in the final match was eight to one.

All of these fine performances, and many others not mentioned here, are an inspiration to all of us, including younger blind boys who one day hope to be on the team. Each achievement of a blind individual aids all of the sightless. The public is slowly learning that there are athletic activities and occupations in which blind people compete on an equal basis with seeing individuals.

Bowlers

There are thousands of visually handicapped bowlers in the United States. Many of the sightless bowlers take a set position at the foul line, while others bring their portable guide rails and use the regular four-step approach. Normally, a partially seeing bowler will knock down twenty-five to thirty more pins than will a sightless contestant. Thus, the difference may not be as great as one might expect.

A high single game of 256 has been bowled by two totally blind men. About twenty years ago a sightless bowler (name unknown), from the New York Lighthouse posted this score, which had also been rolled in 1942 by George McDonald of Oakland, California. For a number of years the latter gave hundreds of public demonstrations of his bowling skill.

In the records of the American Blind Bowling Association, the highest single game by a sightless bowler is 211 bowled by Joe Feinberg of Brooklyn. The high single game for a partially sighted male is 289, turned in by W. Miller of Lancaster, Pennsylvania. Jenny Reeves of Oregon holds the Association record for sightless female bowlers with 165 pins, while partially sighted N. Money has posted 209 for a female record.

High averages in the American Blind Bowling Association for partially seeing, male and female are, V. Augelli of Scranton, 174 and C. Bratt, Fort Wayne, 140. For the totally blind, the high average for males, 144, is held by P. Johnson of Huntington, West Virginia, while the high average for females, 105, is held by A. Burmeister of Chicago.

Totally blind fifty-three-year old Joe Feinberg rolled a three-game series of 580 in 1964. The scores were 184, 202 and 194. What's more he doesn't use a guide rail to bowl. However, Joe gets plenty of practice, as he bowls about twenty games a day in Brooklyn.

A twenty-nine-year old blind bowler, Jenny Reeves of Oregon, was the talk of the 1965 International Bowling Congress Tournament held in Portland, Oregon. She bowled a three-game series or 454, and she did it without a guide rail. A scorekeeper tells her what pins are left standing after her first ball in a frame. She lines up for the next shot by pacing away from the ball return. Miss Reeves helped her Tri-City Team win some prize money. It is interesting to note that all her teammates had normal vision.

Golfers

Golf pros have always told their pupils: "Keep your eye on the ball." Blind men have discovered that this rule is not absolutely necessary. For eighteen holes, a few blind golfers have shot in the 80's, while several have scores under 100. One of the latter is Bob Allman, Secretary of the United States Blind Golfers' Association, who has shot 98 for eighteen holes on two different occasions. It will be remembered that he was the first sightless athlete in the country to win a varsity letter in a college sport—wrestling. Bob Allman would be the first to tell you that during a golf match a blind man's coach is very important. (See page 99.)

Charles Boswell of Birmingham, Alabama, is the outstanding blind golfer in the United States and Canada and probably the world. For fifteen consecutive years, 1948 to 1962, he won the National Tournament for Blind Golfers. The scores usually fluctuated between 204 and 214 for thirty-six holes. Boswell usually exceeds 225 yards with his tee shots. Charles Boswell, who once played football in the Rose Bowl before losing his vision in World War II, had never swung a golf club before the casualty. He now runs an insurance agency in Birmingham and has a sports program on a local radio station.

Between 1938, when the United States Blind Golfers' Tournament originated, and 1946, Clint Russell of Duluth, Minnesota, dominated the event with his fine golfing. The 1962 tournament, held in Atlanta, was won by Joe Lazaro of Waltham, Massachusetts, with a score of 208. The last tournament was held in 1963 in White Plains, New York. The thirty-six-hole event was won with a score of 208 by Claude Pattimore of Canada.

George "Specs" Toporcer is another athlete who turned to golf upon becoming blind at the age of fifty-two. His diamond career took him from New York City sandlot baseball to the St. Louis Cardinals and included the Boston Red Sox, the Chicago White Sox and a place in the International League's Hall of Fame. George Toporcer had played golf before he lost his vision, but he had to learn the game all over again. Usually his scores are a little over 100 for eighteen holes. Since becoming blind, George Toporcer has written many sports stories and traveled thousands of miles to speak on baseball.

A blind man is spared the hazard of looking at trees and creeks, but there are other disadvantages. A low flying plane or a brisk wind can throw a blind golfer's timing off. In common with other golfers, most blind men pull up the head at the end of the swing. Since it is not the eagerness to see the result of the shot, it would appear that this is a mechanical flaw in shoulder action. Blind golfers are unable to see their good shots, but they don't have to look at their bad ones either.

Crew

Perhaps the most recent blind athlete to make a collegiate crew is John Kavanaugh. He was stroke for the number two freshman crew for Stanford University in 1963. One highlight of the season was a victory over a crew from the university of Southern California.

Another blind athlete to make the crew was Don Morgan of Cornell University. He was stroke for one of the crews in 1931.

In June 1955 Princeton's first blind athlete graduated with honors. By the unanimous vote of the Princeton Varsity Oarsmen, Oral Miller was designated as the recipient of the Lyman Biddle Rowing Medal, which is annually conferred upon the senior who throughout the year has shown the best sportsmanship and done the most for rowing.

Although Oral Miller did not make the first crew, he worked long hours before, during and after practice. He was trying to perfect himself in a sport he had never attempted before coming to Princeton. This 6ft 4in 190-pound giant succeeded in winning the admiration of all those connected with rowing at Princeton.

Since perfect timing is a basis of good crew performance, and blindness is not a handicap, it might be expected that more visually handicapped men would report for the sport. Of course, one must usually be over 6 ft tall and weigh 190 pounds or more.

Hikers

Every two years about a dozen boys from the California School for the Blind have completed a 20-mile hike in one day. In 1964 one of these boys found that this was not challenging enough, because he felt strong after the walk of 20 miles led by the writer. This fifteen-year old partially sighted boy, Russell Hubley, carried out an idea of his own. In one day he walked 50 miles on a circular road on the campus of the California School for the Blind and covered the distance in seventeen hours.

In the summer of 1965, totally blind Stephen Hanamura, David Kallinger and Ricky Peterson hiked from the rim of the Grand Canyon down to the Colorado River, 5,000 feet below. The round trip of 22 miles was completed with a sighted companion, Robert McMullen. The Californians made the trip in twelve hours. The hike was a result of Grand Canyon hikes made by some students of the Arizona School for the Blind, (See page 38). Perhaps other blind individuals will accept these challenges in hiking and other sports.

Colette Richard, a twenty-seven-year old blind French woman has made twenty-three major underground explorations, climaxing her adventures by spending a night in the caverns of Saint-Gaudens, France.

Track and Field

On Veterans Day, 1960, Richard McCauley, formerly of Perkins, placed third in a three-mile cross-country race. There were twenty-five high school and college runners in the race. His time was a very good fourteen minutes and fifty-four seconds. This partially sighted man has run well in several 10-mile races, and once ran 18 miles in the famous Boston Marathon.

In 1965, Dick Chapman, a senior at Perkins School for the Blind, finished forty-third in a field of eighty starters in the annual Road Race from Lexington to Cambridge. He held onto the elbow of Claude Ellis, assistant principal. Ellis finished 110th out of 440 starters in the 1965 Boston Marathon. Richard Chapman trained for his big test by running ten miles once a week and from two to five miles each of the other days mainly on the indoor track in the Perkins gym.

The three athletes about to be mentioned have some useful vision. Chauncey Hahn high jumped 6 ft 1 in for Washington State College in 1938. In 1942 Robert Mosher won the Michigan Class D high school quarter-mile championship with a time of 52.3 seconds. He then earned a place on a very good Michigan State University track team. Charles Buell was a member of the 1934 team which won second place in the Southern California Junior College Championship Cross-Country Race held on the challenging three and a half mile course of the University of California at Los Angeles.

Football

From time to time, partially seeing football players become outstanding stars. Such was the case with Alex Karras, All-American at Iowa University and later with the Detroit Lions. Without glasses he cannot see very well, but there is certainly nothing wrong with his football playing. He was once heard to say: "A blur doesn't look so scary."

Alvin Forader, partially sighted, played freshman football at Wesleyan University in Connecticut in 1960. He was a stellar performer as a defensive middle guard.

During the fall of 1954 Earl Monlux played guard well for the University of Washington football team. Earl is very nearsighted and must wear contact lenses. Even then he has difficulty in seeing any great distance.

Bill Turnebaugh, with less than 20/200 vision, was a star lineman for Auburn for three seasons. This 265 pound athlete learned to play defense by studying the way he was blocked by opposing linemen.

Turnebaugh had his grestest thrill in 1952, and it led to victory over Clemson. Late in the game Bill knew by the way he was blocked, that Clemson was throwing a pass. He drifted toward the middle and ran right into the pass thrown by Clemson's Billy Hair. His quick reflexes enabled Turnebaugh to grab the ball and run 10 yd before he was tackled. The interception set up an 18-yd field goal that gave Auburn a 3 to 0 victory.

A team of blind Scottish football players, known as the "Glasgow Rovers," has reportedly never been defeated. Using a ball made of cane, the team has taken on all comers, blind or sighted. Their game called "crab football," is played from a sitting position, and is actually a version of soccer.

Ice Skating

Partially sighted Elwin Kelsey, formerly of the California School for the Blind, and his partner, Christine Simon, won the 1963 Pacific Coast Junior Pairs Championship in ice skating. The following year they won the Pacific Coast Senior Pairs Championship. Also in 1964, Christine and Elwin placed fifth in the National Junior Pairs Championship competition. In 1965 he became a professional by joining the Shipstads and Johnson Ice Follies traveling troupe.

Dancing

Colorful costumes and skillful dancing captured fourth place for the students of the Halifax School for the Blind in competition with sixteen teams in a provincial dance festival held in 1956.

Cheerleading

In 1964 the Western Kentucky State College held a cheerleaders' clinic for 150 schools, including the Kentucky School for the Blind. The blind girls placed fifth in the competition of all the teams.

Baseball

In 1956 the Hudson Guild Neighborhood House won the Manhattan Baseball Championship. The unusual thing about it was that the manager was blind. He was Gus Van Bell, a former baseball player who lost his sight when struck on the head by a pitched ball. A running commentary on the game given to him by his daughter was very helpful.

Fencing

About thirty years ago the New York Guild for the Jewish Blind became interested in fencing. The team of Patrick Conroy, Isidor Hirshberg, Anthony Oliver and William Solomon, all blind, demonstrated their ability against sighted opponents by outfencing most of them.

Alexander Hern, fencing master, introduced a new type of fencing. Briefly, his fencers did not move their whole arms in parry and thrust, but kept them straight out in an "on guard" position. All the side and up and down movements were executed with quick "beats" of the wrist. So quick were they, that they could not be seen. Here, touch is important in finding an adversary's foil. This sense is usually highly developed in blind individuals. They perceive and sometimes even anticipate the strokes of an adversary. When blind fencers lose the opposing blade, they take the offensive. Their immediate attack is the best defense against counterattack. Blind people are usually too fast for the slower, irrational counterattack of sighted opponents.

Gymnastics

Between 1941 and 1944 Edwin Motter won letters in gymnastics every year at the University of California at Los Angeles. He

FIGURE 9. Water skiing at camp—New York Association for the Blind.

specialized in climbing the rope and free exercises. Edwin and his brother, Justus, entered vaudeville with a seven-minute hand balancing act. The fact that the top man was totally blind made each performance an outstanding attraction in the eyes of the public. In five years they appeared in all of the big night clubs, stadiums and other sports arenas in southern California. When Justus was drafted into the Army, Edwin decided to enroll at a school of religion. Today he uses his athletic ability to win young people to the church.

In 1966 partially sighted Tom Bruce won a letter in gymnastics on a championship University of California team in Berkeley. The 5 ft 8 in, 128 lb sophomore shows much promise of future development on the long horse and horizontal bar.

Swimming

King Nawahi, a blind musician, entertained many of the returning veterans of World War II in southern California hospitals. Finding that many sightless veterans were despondent, he decided to prove that blindness is not an insurmountable handicap. On September 1st, 1946, King Nawahi swam from Catalina to Cabrillo on the mainland. The official time for the 26-mile swim was twenty-two hours and fourteen minutes. A current held him off shore for six hours. The greatest hardship suffered during the swim was the burning, caused by the salt water and the grease. His goggles were lost in the first hour after leaving Catalina.

SUMMARY

Blind people are like sighted people. They can do a great deal if they work hard enough toward a particular end. Let's admire the blind and give them opportunities to lead lives of usefulness. The world needs men who can wrestle triumph from defeat.

APPENDICES

APPENDIX A
WINNING TEAMS OF COMPETITION OF THE EASTERN ATHLETIC ASSOCIATION OF THE BLIND

Year	Wrestling	Track and Field
1947	Overbrook	Virginia
1948	Perkins	unavailable
1949	Virginia	unavailable
1950	Virginia	unavailable
1951	N. Carolina	Kentucky
1952	Virginia	Virginia
1953	Virginia	Virginia
1954	W. Virginia	Pittsburgh
1955	Kentucky	Batavia, N.Y.
1956	Virginia	Pittsburgh
1957	W. Virginia	Connecticut
1958	Overbrook (Tie)	Maryland
	Virginia (Tie)	
1959	Virginia	Maryland
1960	Overbrook	Maryland
1961	W. Virginia	Maryland
1962	Overbrook	Maryland
1963	Overbrook	Overbrook
1964	Virginia	Virginia
1965	Virginia	Overbrook

APPENDIX B
WINNING TEAMS IN COMPETITION OF THE MIDWESTERN ATHLETIC ASSOCIATION OF THE BLIND

Year	Wrestling	Track and Field
1951	Iowa	
1952	Iowa	
1953	New Mexico	
1954	New Mexico	Arkansas
1955	New Mexico	Arkansas
1956	Arkansas	Association split

APPENDIX C
WINNING TEAMS IN COMPETITION OF THE SOUTHWESTERN ASSOCIATION OF SCHOOLS FOR THE BLIND

Year	Wrestling	Track and Field
1956		Arkansas
1957	New Mexico	Texas
1958	New Mexico	Texas
1959	Arkansas	Arkansas
1960	New Mexico	Texas
1961	Tennessee	Texas
1962	Texas	Texas
1963	Texas	Texas
1964	Texas	Texas
1965	Texas	Meet not held

APPENDIX D

WINNING TEAMS IN COMPETITION OF NORTH CENTRAL ASSOCIATION OF SCHOOLS FOR THE BLIND

Year	Class A Wrestling	Class B Wrestling	Track and Field
1956			Illinois
1957	Missouri		Missouri
1958	Missouri		Missouri
1959	Missouri		Missouri
1960	Michigan		Missouri (tie)
			Iowa (tie)
1961	Michigan	Kansas	Iowa
1962	Michigan	Kansas	Michigan
1963	Michigan	Kansas	Missouri
1964	Michigan	Kansas	Missouri
1965	Indiana	Kansas	Missouri

APPENDIX E

WINNING TEAMS IN COMPETITION OF SOUTHEASTERN ASSOCIATION OF SCHOOLS FOR THE BLIND

Year	Girls Track	Boys Track
1958	Unavailable	Unavailable
1959	Louisiana	Florida
1960	Tennessee	Florida
1961	Tennessee	Louisiana
1962	Unavailable	Unavailable
1963	Louisiana	Louisiana
1964	Mississippi	Louisiana
1965	Louisiana	Mississippi

APPENDIX F

WINNING SCHOOLS IN WESTERN DECATHLON FOR BLIND BOYS

Year	Junior Division	Senior Division
1959	Arizona	California
1960	California	California
1961	California	California
1962	Arizona	California
1963	Arizona	Arizona
1964	California	Colorado
1965	Arizona	Arizona

APPENDIX G

WINNING TEAMS IN NATIONAL BOWLING LEAGUE OF SCHOOLS FOR THE BLIND

Year	Open Division	Girls Division	Junior Division
1959	California		
1960	Ohio	Ohio	California
1961	Florida	N. Carolina	California
1962	Florida (tie) Nebraska (tie)	California	California
1963	Missouri (large) S. Dakota (small)	California	California
1964	Ohio (class A) California (class B) Oklahoma (class C) S. Dakota (class D)	Georgia	Georgia
1965	Washington (tie) Oklahoma (tie)	Alabama	California

APPENDIX H

THE PERKINS POINT SYSTEM FOR GIRLS

The Perkins Point System was developed by Carol Wadell. The system is based on the cottage plan of living found at Perkins and a few other schools, but it could easily be adapted for other situations. The plan covers activities for six years, seventh through twelfth grades. The point totals are cumulative over the years for each girl.

Individual tournaments are held in shuffleboard and bowling. First, second and third place individual winners receive 5, 3 and 1 points respectively, while the cottages they represent are given 3, 2 and 1 points. Each cottage is given one quarter point for each girl entering a voluntary tournament or meet.

Cottage tournaments are held in shuffleboard, bowling and softball. The cottages compete in a swim meet, track and field meet and gym meet. The latter two meets are the only compulsory events in the entire program. In these the cottages are scored 9-7-5 for first, second and third places respectively.

Individual points are given for being elected to play day (2), or the cheerleading squad (2), and for being a member of the Girls' Athletic Association (2), or making a team (2). Points are awarded for GAA offices as follows: president (4); vice-president (3); and representative (3).

Type of Activity	Points for Entering or Making Team	Individual	Cottage
Individual tournament	2	5-3-1*	3-2-1
Cottage tournament	2	3-2-1*	5-3-1
Cottage track meet		2-1-½†	9-7-5
Cottage gym meet			9-7-5
Cottage swim meet	2	2-1-½†	5-3-1

*In addition, 1 point is given for each win.
†Points are awarded for the first three place winners in each event.

Awards		Additional Awards
Points	Awards	
5-22	Small letter	Winner of individual tournament—silver cup
23-44	Large letter	Winner of cottage tournament—gold cup
45-64	GAA letter	Second and third place winners—ribbons
65-89	Plaque	Cheerleaders—letter and silver megaphone
90-114	Silver medal	charm
115 and up	Trophy	

Cottage Award

A rotating trophy is awarded to the cottage that accumulates the most cottage points each year. If a cottage wins this award three consecutive years, it is kept by that cottage.

APPENDIX I

ARMY AND NAVY EXERCISES TO IMPROVE POSTURE

1. Swing arms forward and upward to full stretch overhead, and at the same time rise high on the toes. Swing arms sideward and downward slowly and press back hard. At the same time, retract chin and let heels drop to the ground. Avoid an exaggerated arch in the lower back.

2. Stand with fingertips touching shoulders, arms in front of chest and elbows downward. Move upper arms outward and backward, with elbows hugging sides. Retract chin, and attempt to stretch upward. Recover to starting position.

3. Kneel on the mat, bend trunk forward, and place hands behind head. Performer straightens upper back while still leaning forward, presses elbows and head backward, at the same time pulling in chin. Recover to starting position.

4. Sit on the mat with knees raised, trunk bent forward, and arms stretched forward. Still leaning forward, performer swings arms upward and backward, while pulling in chin. Recover to starting position.
5. Stand with arms overhead. Pull arms slowly downward until fists are below shoulder. Pull as though chinning. Recover to starting position.
6. Arms rise from attention to cross each other in front of the body, and up overhead, back in circular motion and down to sides. Rise on toes as arms go up, and inhale.
7. Place the hands clasped behind the head, and go to the left or right in circular outward, downward, sideward and then upward motion. Bend at the diaphragm—not the hips—and suck up the stomach when so doing. The shoulders are relaxed.
8. Hands extended overhead, and arms stiff are brought down to touch legs above knees, chin touching collar bone, and suck up the abdominal muscles as the arms come down.
9. From attention, the arms go out and up to a position behind the head; clasp hands as arms are moved forward over the head, twist the hands, palms out still clasped and then down to sides. Inhale at the beginning of the exercise, and exhale only when exercise is completed and arms are at a position of attention.
10. Extend the arms sidewise at shoulder level; drop the right hand 10 in. and raise the left hand 10 in.; suck up the stomach and lock hips. Reverse the positions.

APPENDIX J
BADGE TESTS FOR TUMBLING

The badge tests listed below were developed by Charles Buell for use with visually handicapped children. The badges add interest to a tumbling program and help to motivate it.

Bear

Ten exercises to equal 30 points. One exercise must be done in rolls, balances, springs, bends and novelties. Three couples must be presented.

Lion

Ten exercises to equal 50 points. To win the lion badge, a student must do three couples and at least one exercise in every class except upstarts.

Deer

Ten exercises to equal 70 points. To win the deer badge, a student must do three couples and at least one exercise in every class except upstarts.

Rolls and Dives

Points	Exercise
2	Forward roll, arms folded
3	Forward roll on one foot without hands
3	Backward roll, arms folded
4	Backward roll on one foot
5	Backward roll on one foot without hands
7	Dive without using hands

Balances
(to be held 10 seconds)

Points	Exercise
1	Balancing on hands, knees at shoulders
3	Head and hand balance
4	Head and hand balance, clap hands
4	Forward roll into head and hand balance
5	Backward roll into head and hand balance
5	Hand balance
6	Walk backwards on hands ten steps
8	Hand walk making turn
9	Press up to hand balance

Springs

Points	Exercise
3	Cartwheel
3	Hand stand, snap down
4	Cartwheel, clicking heels
5	Head and hand spring

Springs (Continued)

Points	Exercise
6	Running hand spring
7	Standing hand spring
7	Hand spring from head and hand balance

Bends

Points	Exercise
3	Back bend rocker
3	Bend forward, touch floor with palms, knees stiff
5	Back bend, touching floor
7	From back bend, turn to face down
7	On hands and knees, touch head with foot
9	Back bend and walk

Somersaults

Points	Exercise
5	Forward somersault, arms interlocked with thrower
5	Backward somersault aided by leg lift from thrower
8	Backward somersault from thrower's thighs
9	Forward somersault
12	Backward somersault

Novelties

Points	Exercise
2	From knees jump to stand
3	Armless sit down and rise
3	Hold wrestler's bridge after flip flop
4	Full knee bend on one leg and rise
5	Jump forward and backward over a wand held in both hands
6	One arm push-up
8	One arm pull-up

Upstarts

Points	Exercise
6	Upstart, hands at shoulders
7	Upstart, arms folded
8	Upstart, from hand balance

Couples, Triples

Points	Exercise
3	Double roll
3	Shoulder mount, stepping on thrower's thigh
3	Hand spring on thrower's knees
4	Knee shoulder balance
4	Hand balance and pull over
4	Hands between legs, pull up to thrower's shoulders
5	Hand spring from thrower's hands, standing on shoulders
5	Neck lifts repeated
6	Back bends double
6	Forward and backward rolls combined
7	Double hand spring
7	Low arm hand balance
7	Triple roll
8	Double cartwheel
8	Double roll hand to foot clasp
9	Low hand to hand balance

APPENDIX K
HIGH SCHOOL WRESTLING HONOR ROLL
1961-1965

The won-lost records listed in the Honor Roll vary from one year to life records. Many of the won-lost records are not available. Champions of an athletic association of schools for the blind are indicated by an asterisk.

1961 HONOR ROLL FOR BLIND HIGH SCHOOL WRESTLERS

Name	School for the Blind	Won-Lost	Achievement in State Meet
*Avila, Adolfo	New Mexico	68-0	
*Bennett, Richard	Maryland		
*Blumenthal, Martin	Minnesota		
*Cole, Mitchell	Tennessee	23-0	Champion, 2 times
*Cook, Russell	W. Virginia		
*Crawford, Dave	Illinois	17-1	
*Elliott, Leroy	Overbrook		
Gray, Richard	Nebraska		2nd in state
McLouth, N.	Michigan		Champion
*Parker, Doug	Michigan		Champion
*Rose, D.	Arkansas		
*Unger, Bill	W. Virginia		
*Williams, Emery	Overbrook		

1962 HONOR ROLL FOR BLIND HIGH SCHOOL WRESTLERS

Name	School for the Blind	Won-Lost	Achievement in State Meet
*Bedard, Pat	Iowa		
*Brewer, Ralph	Tennessee		Champion
*Caffery, Fred	Michigan		
*Carnes, Mac	Kentucky		
*Eller, Ron	N. Carolina		
*Emerson, Roy	N. Mexico		
*Gebbink, Jack	Michigan		
*Gleason, Gary	Michigan	21-1	2nd in state
Lewis, C.	Tennessee		Champion
*Light, P.	Virginia		
*McCauley, R.	Perkins		
*Piel, Jim	Missouri		Champion, 2 times
*Randall, W.	Kansas	20-3	3rd in state
*Sarmiento, J.	Arizona		Champion
*Shaw, Kenny	W. Virginia		

1963 HONOR ROLL FOR BLIND HIGH SCHOOL WRESTLERS

Name	School for the Blind	Won-Lost	Achievement in State Meet
*Adkins, Hubert	Virginia	39-2	3rd in state
Archibeque, D.	Colorado	15-2	
*Baccus, Roger	Ohio	12-2	
*Berry, Woody	Virginia	19-3	2nd in state
*Breeden, James	Tennessee		Champion
*Brezinski, Gerald	Overbrook		
Cammack, D.	Idaho	10-2	4th in state
*Dasher, Orval	Nebraska		Champion, 2 times
Dean, Michael	Indiana	10-0	
Garrett, Ron	Alabama	19-1	Champion
Gevedon, J.	Kentucky	14-4	2nd in state
*Grandberry, Curtis	Michigan		
*Halverson, R.	Iowa	14-2	
*Harris, Al	Michigan	39-5	Champion
Hunley, Alva	Indiana	10-0	
*Phipps, L.	Illinois	72-12	1st district, 1st section
*Rodgers, Ed	Michigan		Champion
Rogenski, G.	Wisconsin	12-2	
*Russek, F.	Overbrook	12-0	
*Sykora, L.	Michigan	43-3	Champion
*Thompson, R,	Tennessee	20-2	Champion
Treher, Tom	California	44-11	
*Watson, J.	Texas	7-1	

1964 HONOR ROLL FOR
BLIND HIGH SCHOOL WRESTLERS

Name	School for the Blind	Won- Lost	Achievement in State Meet
*Alcorn, M.	Michigan		
*Angus, Bland	Virginia	20-2	1st in regional
*Attig, Edward	Overbrook	12-0	
*Bailey, M.	Tennessee	19-2	Champion, 2 times
Belew, Bill	Arizona		3rd in state
*Boehmer, R.	Michigan	18-2	Champion
*Brooks, Charles	Overbrook	22-3	
*Brown, R.	Kansas	20-2	
*Chamberlain, J.	Tennessee	15-0	Champion, 2 times
*Chandler, C.	W. Virginia	12-0	
*Clements, J.	Virginia		2nd in regional
*Creech, Bob	N. Carolina	16-3	2nd in state
*Crockett, Jim	Illinois	35-7	2nd in District
*Frees, J.	Michigan	62-7	3rd in state
*Frees, Lloyd	Michigan	85-4	Champion, 2 times
*Harris, Bob	Ohio	8-1	
*Havis, Odis	Texas	6-0	
Henschel, B.	Wisconsin	12-2	2nd in regional
*Holcombe, Allen	Texas		
Larkin, Stan	Wisconsin	19-3	2nd in regional
*Lundstrum, B.	New Mexico	12-1	
McKinley, J.	Idaho	10-1	1st in district
*Machac, Joe	Texas		
Meysembourg, G.	Wisconsin	17-3	2nd in regional
NeSmith, R.	Alabama	14-1	Champion
*Plumlee, Ken.	Missouri		
*Powell, L.	Michigan	38-7	2nd in state
Rhoton, Don	Arizona		3rd in state
*Ryan, R.	Kansas	20-2	
*Sember, T.	Pittsburgh	25-1	
*Spencer, B.	Virginia		2nd in regional
Tolbert, G.	Virginia		1st in regional
*Voss, Gene	Tennessee		2nd in state
Williams, C.	California	90-14	
Wise, J.	Tennessee	18-2	

1965 HONOR ROLL FOR
BLIND HIGH SCHOOL WRESTLERS

Name	School for the Blind	Won-Lost	Achievement in State Meet
*Barr, Joe	N.Y.I.	27-0	
*Bartee, C.	Ohio	26-2	1st in section
*Brewer, F.	Michigan		
*Brickey, R.	Virginia	15-6	
Brito, P.	New Mexico	32-5	Champion
Coach, Tom	Alabama	32-0	Champion
Covington, G.	Alabama		2nd in state
Cravens, T.	Illinois		3rd in section 2nd in district
Crowe, L.	Kentucky		Champion
Dewberry, J.	Missouri		3rd in state
*Dey, Bobby	Kansas	46-6	1st in district
Fuller, C.	Alabama		2nd in state
*Hardin, J.	Kentucky	36-2	Champion, 4 times
*Honyouti, B.	Arizona		Champion, 4 times
Hopkins, E.	Indiana		
Hubley, R.	California	22-2	
Kallinger, D.	California	28-8	
Kingrey, F.	Nebraska	13-1	
*Kopcho, Larry	Colorado	51-3	
*Lewis, C.	Kansas		
*Neice, Clifford	Indiana		
*Oviatt, D.	Nebraska	18-3	Champion
*Pittman, Wayne	Pittsburgh		
*Repp, Dick	Missouri	18-2	1st in district
Ruschival, A.	Kentucky		Champion, 2 times
Sanchez, G.	New Mexico		2nd in state
*Sword, Ken	W. Virginia		
Taylor, Jim	N. Carolina	16-3	3rd in regional
Vargas, Frank	Arizona	14-0	Champion, 4 times
*Vigil, R.	New Mexico		3rd in state
*Weaver, J.	Arkansas	10-1	
Welch, Steve	California	38-5	
*Wheeler, W.	Maryland	8-0	
*White, Dan	W. Virginia	21-2	
Zorick, P.	Connecticut	10-0	

*Association for the Blind champion.

A SELECTED ANNOTATED BIBLIOGRAPHY
ABOUT THE BLIND AND THE HANDICAPPED

American Association of Instructors of the Blind, 2363 South Spring Avenue, St. Louis, Missouri. The Association publishes four times during the year *The International Journal for the Education of the Blind,* a magazine for teachers and parents of visually handicapped children. A summary of the organization's biennial conventions is published in its *Proceedings.*

American Foundation for the Blind, 15 West 16th Street, New York, New York. The organization publishes ten issues per year of *The New Outlook for the Blind,* a professional magazine for teachers and workers for the blind.

BELENKY, ROBERT: *A Swimming Program for Blind Children.* New York, American Foundation for the Blind, 1955, 44 pp. This is the most complete reference available on swimming for blind children.

BUELL, CHARLES: *Motor Performance of Visually Handicapped Children.* Ann Arbor, Michigan, Edwards Brothers, 1950, 125 pp. (Out of print. Summary available from author.) This is a complete doctoral dissertation describing a study involving 865 blind children in public and residential schools. It is the most extensive study of its kind.

BUELL, CHARLES: *Recreation for the Blind.* New York, American Foundation for the Blind, 1951, 40 pp. The pamphlet deals with many phases of recreation for the visually handicapped, including descriptions of many games and related activities.

DANIELS, A. S., and DAVIES, E. A.: *Adapted Physical Education: Principles and Practice of Physical Education for Exceptional Students.* New York, Harper and Row, 1965, 547 pp. Organization, administration, curriculum, class and individual techniques in physical education for blind and other exceptional students are considered.

FAIT, HOLLIS: *Adapted Physical Education.* Philadelphia, W. B. Saunders, 1960, pp. 113-150. One chapter of the book is devoted to physical education for visually handicapped children. Since some blind children are multiply handicapped, the other deviations discussed will be of value.

FARRELL, GABRIEL: *The Story of Blindness*. Cambridge, Harvard University Press, 1956, 270 pp. The history of the blind, their education and status in society are competently reviewed.

FRAMPTON, M., and MITCHELL, P.: *Camping for Blind Youth*. New York, New York Institute for the Blind, 1949, 139 pp. Many phases of camping for blind children are discussed.

HUNT, VALERIE: *Recreation for the Handicapped*. Englewood Cliffs, New Jersey, Prentice-Hall, 1955, pp. 78-98. One chapter of the book is devoted to blind children. How to carry on various activities is emphasized. The discussion of other handicaps will be found helpful.

LENDE, HELGA: *Books About the Blind*. New York, American Foundation for the Blind, 1953, 357 pp. This comprehensive bibliography covers all important literature on the blind which appeared before 1953.

LOWENFELD, BERTHOLD: *Our Blind Children*. Springfield, Illinois, Charles C Thomas, 1964, 240 pp. An authoritative discussion of a wide range of problems faced by blind children of all ages. Although it likely will be of most value to parents of blind children, the book also will be helpful to social workers and teachers.

POMEROY, J.: *Recreation for the Physically Handicapped*. New York, Macmillan Co., 1964, 382 pp. Community recreation departments, teachers, public health and social welfare personnel will benefit from this book. It is organized around activities, but specific handicaps are mentioned from time to time.

RITTER, CHARLES: *Hobbies for Blind Adults*. New York, American Foundation for the Blind, 1953, 52 pp. The pamphlet covers in some detail a wide variety of hobbies for blind adolescents and adults.

WALKER, LEROY: *Physical Education for the Exceptional Student*. Dubuque, Iowa, W. C. Brown, 1963, 63 pp. Defects covered are cardiac deficiency, polio, cerebral palsy, epilepsy, multiple sclerosis, obesity, arthritis, orthopedic conditions and blindness (two pages).

ZAHL, PAUL (ed.): *Blindness: Modern Approaches to the Unseen Environment*. Princeton, Princeton University Press, 1950, 576 pp. Problems connected with blindness are discussed by specialists in work with the blind.

GENERAL PHYSICAL EDUCATION

American Association of Health, Physical Education and Recreation: *YOUTH FITNESS TEST MANUAL.* Washington, D. C., The Association, a department of the National Education Association, 1965, 80 pp. A description is given of the test most widely used to measure physical fitness of public school children.

American Association of Health, Physical Education and Recreation: *Physical Education for High School Students.* Washington, D. C., The Association, a department of the National Education Association, 1955, 406 pp. Games, sports and recreational activities, skills, strategy, rules and playing areas for a great many activities are discussed.

American National Red Cross, Washington, D. C.: *Teaching Johnny to Swim, Swimming and Diving, Life Saving and Water Safety.* These helpful booklets may be purchased from local branches of the American National Red Cross.

ANDREWS, GLADYS: *Creative Rhythmic Movement for Children.* New York, Prentice-Hall, 1954, 198 pp. This is an excellent help for classroom teachers because of the manner of presentation which brings about the understanding of the origin and benefits of creativity. Concentration is made upon movement as a form of expression.

ANDREWS, G., and others: *Physical Education for Today's Boys and Girls.* Boston, Allyn and Bacon, 1960, 431 pp. Emphasis is placed upon helping teachers get started in a movement-oriented approach to physical education; descriptions are given of a great variety of activities that can contribute to the growth and development of boys and girls in elementary school. Excellent illustrations are included.

ANDREWS, G., and others: *Physical Education for Girls and Women.* Englewood Cliffs, New Jersey, Prentice- Hall, 1963, 263 pp. Activities described which are of particular interest to teachers of blind girls are bowling, dancing, gymnastics, stunts and tumbling, swimming and synchronized swimming and camping. It is an excellent guide for beginning teachers.

ARMBRUSTER, ALLEN, and BILLINGSLEY: *Swimming and Diving.* St. Louis, C. V. Mosby, 1963, 352 pp. Every phase of modern swimming and diving, the training methods, techniques, racing conditions and teaching situations are thoroughly, simply and scientifically discussed. Many illustrations are included.

Athletic Institute, 209 South State Street, Chicago 4, Illinois. Of particular interest to physical educators of the blind are inexpensive pamphlets on wrestling, tumbling, bowling, apparatus activities, gymnastics for girls, swimming, life saving, trampolining and track and field.

BABBITT, D., and HAAS, W.: *Gymnastic Exercises for Girls.* New York, Ronald Press, 1964, 130 pp. Introductory and intermediate phases of apparatus work are covered with special attention to description of skills, teaching hints and spotting. Exercises for balance beam, vaulting apparatus, uneven parallel bars, trampoline and rings are included.

BRESNAHAN, G., TUTTLE, W., and CRETZMEYER, F.: *Track and Field Athletics.* St. Louis, C. V. Mosby, 1964, 424 pp. In its sixth edition, this book has stood the test of time.

California Physical Performance Tests. Sacramento, California State Department of Education, 1962, 45 pp. Five tests make up the battery, three of which may be used without modification for blind children.

DOHERTY, K.: *Modern Track and Field.* Englewood Cliffs, New Jersey, Prentice-Hall, 1963, 557 pp. A leading college coach of thirty years discusses, in a practical way, what he has learned about track and field. Methods of improving performance in various events are stressed.

DRURY, B., and MOLNAR, A.: *Gymnastics for Women.* Palo Alto, California, National Press, 1964, 198 pp. Many illustrations are included in this manual for teachers in the secondary school. Suggestions are made for exhibitions and competitive meets. In addition to apparatus work and trampoline exercises, rhythmic gymnastics are discussed in detail.

FAIT, HOLLIS: *Physical Education for the Elementary School Child.* Philadelphia, W. B. Saunders, 1964, 390 pp. Emphasis is placed upon practical methods for use in situations as they often occur. Descriptions of stunts and tumbling, games and all types of rhythms are included.

FRY, H., and KEENEY, C.: *Elementary Gymnastic Skills Illustrated.* New York, Ronald Press, 1964, 144 pp. A concise, usable teaching aid for the instructor of elementary gymnastic apparatus skills has a series of photographs. It is excellent for beginners in parallel bars, horizontal bar, side horse and rings.

HALL, J. T.: *Dance! A Complete Guide to Social, Folk, and Square Dancing.* Belmont, California, Wadsworth Publishing Co., 1963, 256 pp. Eighty-five of the best known folk dances, thirty-six popular square dances and the fundamentals of soft shoe and tap dancing are described in this comprehensive book. Diagrams, music, and photographs accompany the text.

HALSEY, E., and PORTER, L.: *Physical Education for Children—A Developmental Program.* New York, Holt, Rinehart and Winston, 1963, 449 pp. The authors have developed a text based upon sound principles of child growth and development. The book should be useful to students majoring in physical education as well as serving as a good resource for in-service education.

HARRIS, PITTMAN, and WALLER: *Dance Awhile, A Handbook of Folk, Square and Social Dance.* Minneapolis, Burgess Publishing Co., 1963, 270 pp. Dances are described in simple, direct language with suggestions for the beginning teacher. About 200 dances are covered.

HORNE, V. L.: *Stunts and Tumbling for Girls.* New York, Ronald Press, 1943, 219 pp. This book is an excellent guide to use in selecting and teaching stunts for both boys and girls in both elementary and high school. It gives equipment needed, principal values, descriptions, progressions and safety measures for each stunt.

KEEN, C., SPEIDEL, C., and SWARTZ, R.: *Championship Wrestling.* Annapolis, Maryland, U. S. Naval Institute, 1964, 230 pp. This manual covers every stage of wrestling from beginning to Olympic competition; for individuals, coaches and instructors. There are many illustrations.

KEENEY, C.: *Trampolining Illustrated.* New York, Ronald Press, 1961, 149 pp. Step-by-step learning procedures of fifty elementary and intermediate trampoline exercises are described and clearly shown in photographs.

KIPHUTH, R., and BURKE, H.: *Basic Swimming.* New Haven, Yale University Press, 1958, 125 pp. A book designed primarily to teach people of all ages how to swim well, whatever their skill. These outstanding coaches have included many photographs to illustrate movements.

LA SALLE, D.: *Guidance of Children Through Physical Education.* New York, Ronald Press, 1957, 375 pp. Suggested curricula, classified according to age and grade levels one through six are clearly presented, each with its specific objectives. Activities are described in such a way that an elementary school teacher can make best use of them.

LA SALLE, D.: *Rhythms and Dance for Elementary Schools.* New York,

Ronald Press, 1951, 168 pp. Over 200 rhythms and dances are included with detailed descriptions and music.

LOKEN, N., and WILLOUGHBY, R.: *Complete Book of Gymnastics.* Englewood Cliffs, New Jersey, Prentice-Hall, 1962, 212 pp. A complete range of gymnastics, calisthenics, rope climbing, rope skipping and exhibitions for men and women of all levels are discussed.

MACIS, R.: *Learning How to Wrestle.* Mankato, Minnesota, Creative Educational Society, 1965, 127 pp. In this inexpensive book the emphasis is on sound basic fundamentals illustrated by over 120 action pictures. It is a practical book of coaching methods, techniques and strategy.

MANN, JACK: *Square Dance Manual.* The author, 540 Alcatraz Avenue, Oakland, California, 1961, 49 pp. Dance exercises are arranged in logical order for teaching a fifteen-lesson course in square dancing. Beginning as well as experienced teachers will find the manual helpful.

MILLER, K.: *Track and Field for Girls.* New York, Ronald Press, 1964, 117 pp. Skills essential to a successful, well-rounded girls' track and field program for beginners as well as those with higher levels of ability are thoroughly covered. Included are many drawings and photographs.

National Collegiate Athletic Bureau, Box 757, Grand Central Station, New York 17, New York. The annual guides published for wrestling and track and field are particularly valuable for physical educators of the blind.

RATHBONE, J., and HUNT, V.: *Corrective Physical Education.* Philadelphia, W. B. Saunders, 1965, 267 pp. This thorough book on corrective physical education may be helpful to teachers of blind children. In its seventh edition, this standard book presents up-to-date information.

SMITH, HOPE: *Water Games.* New York, Ronald Press, 1962, 95 pp. There are 130 water games presented which instill confidence in beginning to experienced swimmers.

SPARKS, RAY: *Wrestling Illustrated.* New York, Ronald Press, 1960, 135 pp. Every move is clearly illustrated by photographs. An outline for thirty lessons is included.

SZYPULA, GEORGE: *Tumbling and Balancing for All.* Dubuque, Iowa, W. C. Brown, 1957, 161 pp. The learning of tumbling could not be made easier. Photographs are extensively used by the author who is a four-time NAAU tumbling champion.

TURNER, MARGARET: *Dance Handbook.* Englewood Cliffs, New Jersey, Prentice-Hall, 1959, 136 pp. Features all forms of dance generally taught in schools today. Discusses fundamentals and source materials including records.

VAN HAGEN, W., DEXTER, G., and WILLIAMS, J.: *Physical Education in the Elementary School.* Sacramento, California State Department of Education, 1951. 1008 pp. (Can be purchased only from publisher.) This is a comprehensive and practical guide for the elementary school teacher in conducting physical education activities. Detailed descriptions are given of games, rhythms and dances, relays and stunts.

VANNIER, M., and FOSTER, M.: *Teaching Physical Education in Elementary Schools.* Philadelphia, W. B. Saunders, 1963, 429 pp. Descriptions of activities which have been tried and proven successful in elementary schools are included. There are chapters on rhythms and dance, stunts and tumbling, classroom quiet games and restricted programs for atypical children.

VANNIER, M., and FAIT, H.: *Teaching Physical Education in the Secondary School.* Philadelphia, W. B. Saunders, 1964, 480 pp. This book covers facilities, procedures, program planning and evaluation, methods, help for new teachers, coeducational activities, isometric exercises, figure control, cheerleading and drill teams. There are 192 illustrations.

VERMES, H., and VERMES, J.: *The Collier Quick and Easy Guide to Bowling.* New York, Collier Books, 1963, 127 pp. The information needed to start a program of bowling is contained in this inexpensive, extensively illustrated book. Suggestions are made for beginners as well as those who have some skill.

WELLS, K.: *Posture Exercise Handbook.* New York, Ronald Press, 1963, 88 pp. An up-to-date scientific approach to improved appearance and physical fitness is presented. The development of balance, agility, strength and coordination is covered in the order recommended for individual exercise sessions.

INDEX

Western Pennsylvania School for the
   Blind, 21, 23, 24, 26
West Virginia School for the Deaf and
   Blind, 28, 34, 42
Wheelbarrow relay, 139
Winds, 53
Winter sports, 98
Wisconsin School for the Visually Handi-
   capped, 28, 35, 41

Wrestling
   description of, 86, 87
   history, 28, 34, 39
   in curriculum, 46, 60, 61
   leaders in, 37
   outstanding wrestlers, 185-191

Y

Young, Charles, 37, 141